Master of the Crowd

8 Proven Ways to Captivate Any Audience

By Jamal "DJ Mal-Ski" McCoy

Table of Contents

Master: (mas·ter), noun

1. One having control

2. An artist, performer, or player of consummate
    skill

Master: (mas·ter), adjective

1. Having chief authority: dominant

2. Skilled, proficient

Master: (mas·ter), verb

1. To gain a thorough understanding of

2. To become skilled or proficient in the use of

Dear Reader,

Have you ever watched someone step in front of a crowd and instantly command the room, like they were born for that moment? You know the type. Their voice cuts through the noise. Their energy sets the tone. People lean in and are captivated, not just by hearing them, but *experiencing* them.

I'll let you in on a little secret: That kind of presence isn't a talent. It's a skill. And it's one *you* can learn.

I wrote *Master of the Crowd* for a very specific type of person—a person like you.

Whether you're a DJ aiming to ignite a stadium, a business leader pitching a vision, a teacher exploring ways to hold attention in the classroom, a speaker stepping on stage, or even a parent focused on connecting with your kids, this book is your playbook for capturing attention and keeping it.

Here's the truth—in any room, with any crowd, your ability to engage, influence, and leave an impact determines your success.

The difference between being heard and being unforgettable lies in one simple skill:

Mastering The Crowd.

This book shares eight proven strategies I've learned through years of commanding stages, stadiums, classrooms, corporate events, and even airspace—yes, airspace. As a U.S. Air Force air traffic controller turned world-touring DJ, I've lived in high-pressure environments where presence, precision, and authority were nonnegotiable. I've hosted some of the world's biggest events and performed with legends like Stevie Wonder and Snoop Dogg. And throughout every stage of my life, from childhood cafeteria rap battles to stadium roars, I've learned that energy isn't something you react to—it's something you create.

Inside these pages, you'll find the real techniques I've used to go from nervous first impressions to unforgettable mic-drop moments. You'll learn how to do the following:

- Command attention like a playground whistle.

- Decode audiences to eliminate fear and hesitation.[1]

- Master first impressions that build instant trust and respect.

- Use music, psychology, and energy to engage any crowd.

---

[1] This kind of presence isn't a talent—it's a skill. According to research in psychology and neuroscience, presence and charisma are trainable behaviors that can be developed with intention and feedback. Amy Cuddy, *Presence: Bringing Your Boldest Self to Your Biggest Challenges* (Little, Brown, and Company, 2015).

- Leverage surprise, subtle rebellion, and emotional connection to keep people locked in.

This isn't just theory—it's tested. From leading 8,000-plus college students at the University of Southern California's Splash Bash to teaching top corporate executives how to control room energy to guiding fighter pilots through high-risk airspace. And these principles *work*.

So, who is this book for?

It's for the **high-energy leader** who's ready to level up their ability to connect.

It's for the **rising DJ or host** who wants to turn crowds into believers.

It's for the **coach, teacher, or speaker** who needs to make messages stick.

It's for the **parent, entrepreneur, influencer, or boss** who wants to be unforgettable, not by being the loudest but by being the most intentional.

If you've ever felt overlooked, talked over, or unsure how to break through the noise, *this book is for you.*

Let me be clear: Mastering the crowd isn't about controlling people. It's about creating experiences people never forget.

It's about turning nervous energy into magnetic energy. It's about knowing how to shift a room just by walking into it.

This is your moment. Your stage. Your classroom. Your locker room. Your meeting.

Whatever your "crowd" looks like, you can own it. Not with force but with clarity, confidence, and energy.

So turn the page. Lean in. And get ready to step into your next level.

It's time to stop hoping people will pay attention, and start mastering the crowd. Let's begin.

—DJ Mal-Ski

Chapter 1

Mastering Captivation: "Be the Whistle"

"You don't need to be the loudest voice, just the one
they trust..."

The Playground

On my first day at Locust Elementary School, I experienced bullying firsthand. What happened that day wasn't just a childhood memory—it was the first lesson I ever learned about commanding attention, holding it, and transforming a crowd. It's a lesson that has shaped my experience on every stage I've stepped on and affected every audience I've ever addressed.

The lunchtime bell had just rung. I walked out of my classroom, through the quad area, and onto the playground, stepping into what seemed like a completely different world. The playground buzzed with excitement. A joyful tone of chatter and laughter greeted me as I walked into the sunlit schoolyard. Kids scattered everywhere, their energy radiating through the air. The excitement was unmistakable, but most eyes were focused in one direction.

Carnot Ledbetter—a sixth grader and self-proclaimed Master of the Playground—stood on a planter. He was tall, buff, and charismatic, mesmerizing the crowd of students with his comedy and rap skills. The students surrounding him cheered and laughed, hanging on to his every word. As I walked up, rocking my swap-meet-fresh LBC hat and new shoes, Carnot's gaze locked onto me. He finished a line in his rap and hurled some choice words at me that I didn't appreciate. He made an immediate and authoritative first impression. Wait—was this Pick on the New Kid Day?

As Carnot's words hit me, it seemed as if the whole playground heard them and laughed. Although I was just a fifth grader, I knew I couldn't stand by silently. After all, this wasn't just my first day of school—it was my first day in a new city, facing new kids with new playground rules. Was this what school was going to be like every day? Where I was from, in Long Beach, you didn't back down from a fight, but I was so nervous and caught off guard that I was shaking. Should I respond? I didn't know what this crowd liked. What if they didn't like me? What if I said something that was too disrespectful?

Was I going to have to squabble with this dude for trying to roast me?

(Squabble: a noisy quarrel about something petty)

(Roast: insulting someone for comedic effect)

Despite my fear and my lack of understanding of playground hierarchy, I straightened my LBC hat and, with as much charisma as I could muster, fired back. It was a risk, but one I felt was worth taking. The crowd responded with a collective "Whoa!" Suddenly, all eyes were on the short new kid from Long Beach.

Carnot responded with more roasts aimed at me—my height, my weight, and whatever other insults he could conjure up on the spot. Each one was sharper than the last. The flurry of insults came as fast and furious as a Dominic Toretto quarter mile, and I wasn't prepared for the sheer speed of it all.

As Carnot leaned into his attack, I noticed something: The crowd had doubled in no time, and they weren't just watching—they were captivated. Dozens of kids had now abandoned their games and activities on the playground to form a massive concert-like circle around us, their faces full of either shock or amusement as Carnot continued his verbal assault.

Fueled by frustration, I fired back again. This time, my words carried all the emotions of being uprooted from my home, my friends, and my life in Long Beach. Carnot had unknowingly become the target of my pent-up anger. I was hitting him with roasts about everything: his appearance, his clothes, his hair. However, when I commented on his ProWing gym shoes, saying that "they were so old the feathers must've been on Noah's ark," the crowd erupted with laughter and cheers. But Carnot didn't. All of a sudden, his face darkened, his playful smirk disappeared, and he jumped down from the planter, aggressively heading toward me. I was terrified.

The crowd parted for Carnot as if he were Moses and they were the Red Sea. His fists were clenched, his stride deliberate. He was actually much taller than I had thought. My heart sank as I realized just how bad this might get. Still, I dropped my book bag and Pee-Chee folder (yes, I said "Pee-Chee folder"), determined not to back down. My bravado might have remained intact on the outside, but inside, my heart was pounding like a bass drum.

Carnot reached out his hands to grab me by the shirt and pulled me closer, ready to rip my head off. I closed my eyes, bracing for the worst. And then—something miraculous happened. An illustrious miracle, one that was just as glorious and powerful as I imagined the sound that created the heavens was. Its beauty, majesty, and timeliness cannot be overstated! It was the sound of a playground whistle.

The Power of the Whistle

The whistle.

Sharp, piercing, and commanding, it shattered the chaos like the opening note of a symphony. This was no ordinary sound. It carried the kind of authority that transcended words, reaching into the deepest recesses of every kid's mind.

Carnot froze. I froze. The crowd froze.

For a split second, the playground was silent, as if the world itself had paused to obey the call of that whistle.

Now, before I can continue, we must talk for a moment about the power and authority of a playground whistle. In the late 1980s, the playground whistle wasn't just a sound, it was a symbol of universal authority. It didn't just exist on the playground. It was a constant presence on soccer fields, basketball courts, and football fields. It was the sound that stopped plays, reset the action, and demanded immediate attention. Students, athletes, and teachers all knew its power. From the first day of preschool, we were conditioned to stop, look, and listen whenever it blew.

That whistle didn't just stop Carnot; it stopped everything. The chaos, the fight, the tension—it all evaporated. The playground itself seemed to hold its breath, captivated by the whistle's power. Even Carnot, the self-proclaimed Master of the Playground, couldn't resist its authority.

Mr. Horn stood there, whistle in hand, his wiry frame radiating authority. He didn't have to say a word. The whistle had spoken for him.

And in that moment, something clicked in my mind. If a single sound could command attention, interrupt chaos, and hold an entire playground of elementary school students in its grip, then mastering that kind of power—*being the whistle*—was something I needed to figure out.

The whistle wasn't just a tool of authority; it was a symbol of order amid chaos, a rallying call that made everyone stop and pay attention. The way it brought clarity to the confusion of the playground showed me something profound: It's not about being the loudest or most intimidating. It's about having the right presence at the right time.

Mr. Horn's Insightful Spark

It wasn't until later that I realized how much I owed to Mr. Horn. He was the wiry, no-nonsense teacher who had blown the whistle and defused the fight. After stepping in and saving me from needing facial reconstruction surgery, he and another teacher escorted me and Carnot to the principal's office. Once we arrived,

Mr. Horn didn't just describe what had happened to our principal. He said something that changed the course of the day—and maybe my life.

"These two boys," he said to Principal Velasquez, "have something special. They've got talent. If we channel it the right way, they could really bring something positive to this school."

That one comment sparked an idea in Principal Velasquez's mind, but it wasn't just about what had happened on the playground. Principal Velasquez had been dealing with a persistent issue that had been plaguing the school: the brand-new cafeteria.

The school had recently invested in a beautiful cafeteria, complete with new tables, upgraded food options, and a design meant to foster community and connection. But it wasn't working. Students were either rushing through lunch or skipping it entirely, eager to get out onto the playground as quickly as possible. The cafeteria, despite its shiny exterior, often sat half empty.

Principal Velasquez had been brainstorming ways to draw students in and create a sense of community. He wanted lunch to be more than just a time to eat. He wanted it to be a chance for connection, and he wanted the cafeteria to be a place where students could feel engaged with one another. But he hadn't been able to crack the code.

That's when Mr. Horn's comment about our "talent" lit a spark.

Principal Velasquez began to see an opportunity to address two issues at once—to manage the fallout from our playground showdown and breathe life into the cafeteria.

"For the next two weeks, you two are going to perform during lunch in the cafeteria," he said. "Poems, jokes, raps—whatever you want, as long as it's clean. But if you cuss, skip a day,

or fight each other, you'll be suspended and possibly expelled. No exceptions." Our punishment wasn't just a consequence—it was also a solution.

Principal Velasquez paused, letting the weight of the decision settle in. "You both caused chaos today, but maybe you can use that same energy to bring people together."

From Punishment to Performance

That following Monday, it was like the Super Bowl on campus. Everyone, including teachers, was talking about our highly anticipated lunchtime duel. In the bathroom, I had overheard some kids saying, "Carnot is going to kill that new Long Beach kid," then heard another kid say, "I kind of like the new Long Beach kid, and I hope he wins."

So, the lunch bell rang. The time had come. The cafeteria was packed wall to wall. We each finished eating early and stepped up on the riser. Carnot was wearing a T-shirt with the sleeves cut off to show his muscles. I had my standard LBC hat and fresh kicks.

As we both stepped up on that riser and faced each other, it was like the start of a title fight. The entire school had found their way inside this tiny cafeteria and was waiting with excitement. Even the teachers were standing along the back against the walls, waiting with anticipation to see what would happen. The cool kids, who used to rush through lunch to get back outside, now claimed their own table, eager to watch what would be the first of two weeks of performances.

It wasn't until I was standing on that cafeteria riser, facing Carnot, who was way bigger, cooler, and more popular than I was, that I remembered that whistle. I realized that I wanted to be that whistle—captivating, cutting through the noise, and commanding attention. I couldn't compete with Carnot's size or, at that time, his abilities. This was his campus and his audience. All I could do was hope to become the attention grabber, hope I could say something that would make everyone stop and listen.

Principal Velasquez had made it clear that Carnot wasn't allowed to touch me physically, so I felt free to go as far as I needed to go. I had spent the better part of Friday evening and the entire weekend getting to know as many students and teachers as I could. I'd asked them questions about all kinds of things: their favorite candies, favorite cartoons, favorite singers or rappers. I'd even asked them what they liked and hated about the school. At that point, I had decoded my audience and felt as if I knew every student and teacher in the cafeteria. Armed with this information, I felt my nervousness disappear. I was ready.

So, I decided I would set the tone early. I started out with a roast, saying Carnot's outfit was older than the cafeteria ladies' wigs.

The crowd immediately responded, "Whoa!" It was the loudest audience I had ever heard.

Carnot then replied, saying my head was so big it couldn't even fit in Fat Tommy's belly. The crowd lit up! "Wow!" And it got even louder. We couldn't believe the crowd was this loud!

I looked at Carnot, and he looked back at me, smiling, and I think we realized in that very moment that this wasn't about us battling any longer. This was about them—the crowd.

What was meant to be consequences became the highlight of every school day. Carnot and I didn't just entertain the cafeteria—we transformed it into the place to be. Students who normally avoided lunch started showing up early to ensure they got seats. Teachers who dreaded lunch duty began trading for it.

The cafeteria staff, along with some of the special education kids, even designed handmade posters for us.

Performing every day taught us how to captivate and hold attention. It wasn't just about grabbing the spotlight—it was about connecting with the crowd, reading their energy, and giving them something to care about. We experimented with jokes, rhymes, and stories, learning what worked and what didn't. It was an early lesson in crowd psychology: when to push, when to pull back, and how to adapt on the fly.

By the end of the two weeks, the cafeteria had become more than a place to eat—it was a place of community. Kids from different grades, who might never have spoken to each other otherwise, were laughing and bonding over our performances. Even the teachers started to notice a shift in the school's atmosphere. What had begun as a punishment had turned into a unifying experience and a seed of what my life and career would eventually center around. We had become the whistle.

Foreshadowing the Journey

Looking back, those playground showdowns and cafeteria performances weren't just childhood moments—they were the foundation of everything I would learn about engaging and captivating audiences. They showed me the power of timing, presence, and connection. They taught me that commanding attention isn't about dominating a space. It's about understanding the people within it.

The playground and cafeteria taught me how to hold an audience's attention. But years later, in one of the most high-pressure environments in the world, I would learn what it truly meant to command it. In the United States Air Force, controlling attention wasn't just about entertainment—it was about survival.

The Playground Was My First Lesson—the Air Force Was My Masterclass

It didn't take a loud, booming voice or a towering presence to steal the spotlight that day. I saw that real command comes from control.

Mr. Horn wasn't bigger than Carnot. He wasn't the loudest person on the playground. But when he blew that whistle, everyone stopped.

At that moment, I understood that one clear sound, one undeniable presence, could override chaos.

I didn't know it at the time, but that lesson—how one clear signal could override chaos— would later define my role in one of the most high-pressure jobs in the world: controlling the skies.

When you're an air traffic controller in the United States Air Force, your voice isn't just guiding people's attention—your voice is the difference between order and catastrophe, between safety and disaster.

Be the Whistle: Lessons from Air Traffic Control

Before I was commanding stadiums, before I was rocking arenas, and before I was leading thousands in energy and engagement, I was doing something far more intense: I was an air traffic controller in the United States Air Force.

If you've never heard it before, hear it from someone who lived it: Air traffic control isn't just high pressure—it's consistently ranked as one of the most high-stress professions in the world.[2] And there's a reason for that. In this job, precision isn't a luxury. It's the line between order and chaos. Between hundreds of lives landing safely…and catastrophe. Every call, every phrase, every pause carries weight. There's no room for guessing. Just clarity, control, and confidence—on demand.

At Keesler Air Force Base in Biloxi, Mississippi, I trained in the most rigorous program imaginable, designed to produce

---

[2] Joanna Zambas, "The 30 Most Stressful Jobs (and How Much They Pay)," CareerAddict, last updated June 22, 2022, https://www.careeraddict.com/stressful-jobs.

controllers who could handle intense pressure and make splitsecond decisions with absolute clarity. But what set air traffic control apart from any other job? We didn't just learn procedures. We had to master an entirely new language.

The Power of Phraseology: Saying More with Less

In air traffic control, every second matters. When you're speaking to pilots—sometimes 30 at a time—you don't have time for casual conversation. You don't have time for "Uh, hey, can you maybe turn left when you get a chance?" No.

Air traffic controllers speak in something called "phraseology," a language specifically designed to convey maximum information in minimum words. Every term has a precise meaning, and every instruction must be clear, quick, and unambiguous.

For example, instead of saying:

"Hey, Eagle 354, I see you're getting close to another aircraft, so if you could just kinda slow down and maybe fly lower, and also maybe turn right when you can, that'd be great, you'll be landing soon."

A controller would say:

"Eagle 354, reduce speed, maintain 300 knots. Turn right, heading 270. Descend and maintain 5,000. Expect clearance in two minutes." Boom. Clear, quick, effective.

This is exactly what being the whistle means.

You don't have to be the loudest person in the room.

You don't have to dominate with force.

You just have to be the one who cuts through the noise with absolute authority.

Controlling Chaos: My Time at Nellis Air Force Base

After training at Keesler Air Force Base, I was stationed at Nellis Air Force Base in Las Vegas, Nevada—one of the busiest air force bases in the world. This wasn't just any base. This was where the best fighter pilots in the military trained for combat.

My role? Radar approach controller.

Unlike a tower controller—who manages takeoffs, landings, and taxiing within five miles of the airport—I was responsible for thousands of miles of airspace. If you can imagine how many planes are in the sky at any given moment within thousands of miles, you can begin to understand the level of precision required for this job.

Every morning, pilots would depart to training airspace miles away to run their combat drills. But once training ended, that's when my real work began.

All at once, dozens of fighter pilots from all over the sky—50 pilots or more—would check in on the frequency, requesting clearance to come home and land. Imagine this:

Fifty voices, all speaking at once.

Multiple high-speed aircraft, all moving in different directions.

Numerous planes, each of which had to be separated by at least three miles and 1,000 feet.

Dozens of pilots, all relying on one voice to bring them home safely.

That voice was mine. In those moments, I had to be the whistle.

I wasn't screaming. I wasn't competing with their voices. I wasn't adding to the noise. I was cutting through it.

Calm.

Clear.

Commanding.

When I spoke, the pilots stopped speaking. When I gave instructions, they followed without hesitation. Because in air traffic control, just like in mastering a crowd, uncertainty is a weakness. Clarity is power.

Authority in the Midst of Rank: The Dichotomy of Command

One of the most fascinating dynamics in military air traffic control is that every single pilot in the sky outranked me.

I was an enlisted airman—but the pilots I was directing? All commissioned officers. Every single one of them had more rank and more authority on paper. But when it came to airspace, communication, and the safe return of all aircraft, I was in control.

This created a strange but powerful dichotomy.

I had to assert authority over people who technically outranked me.

I had to command respect, not demand it.

I had to control the chaos with absolute clarity—without arrogance.

And you know what? That's exactly what commanding an audience is like.

It doesn't matter if you're speaking to executives, athletes, artists, or students. The size of the audience doesn't matter. Your authority comes from your ability to direct the moment with clarity and confidence.

The Science of Getting People Home

Controlling airspace isn't just about issuing commands—it's about creating a sequence.

Imagine 30 fighter jets all checking in at the same time. My job wasn't just to manage the airspace. It was also to create a sequence, control the flow, and guide every single pilot home safely and efficiently.

There are no stop signs in the sky. No red lights. No intersections.

It's all about flow, sequencing, and delivering instructions that even the most elite pilots don't question.

When you're in front of an audience, it's the same principle.

1. **You're sequencing their attention.**

2. **You're setting the pattern for their focus.**

3. **You're leading them safely through an experience.**

Mr. Horn and the Whistle: The Ultimate Connection

This is why the concept of being the whistle is so powerful. Mr. Horn didn't yell, flex, or intimidate. Using the whistle, he signaled, and the playground snapped to order. Just like in air traffic control, it's not about volume or status, it's about the authority that whistle represented.

And that's exactly how you should approach every audience you stand in front of.

You don't have to scream.

You don't have to have the most aggressive voice in the room.

You don't have to outrank your audience.

You just have to be the voice that cuts through the noise. The one they trust to lead them through the moment. The one that delivers clarity, structure, and a sense of control.

Respectfully control your airspace—but do it with empathy.

Be the whistle.

From Fighter Pilots to Stadium Crowds: Authority Is in Your Delivery

Like I said, when I was in that radar control facility at Nellis Air Force Base, managing dozens of elite fighter pilots, I wasn't the highest-ranking person in the conversation. Every single one of the pilots outranked me.

But when it came to airspace, my rank didn't matter. What mattered was the way I communicated. If I sounded hesitant, if I lacked precision, if I let my voice get lost in the noise—they wouldn't trust me.

The same is true every time you step in front of an audience.

Whether you're speaking to a crowd of 10 or 10,000, leading a business meeting, or even just introducing yourself in a room full of people, it's not about how important you are on paper.

It's about how much authority you carry in your presence.

If you sound unsure, people hesitate to follow you.

If you talk too much, people tune out.

If you master tone, timing, and precision, people listen—every time.

That's the power of being the whistle.

Remaining Authority-Focused

We've covered a lot in this chapter. We've gone from a playground lesson in authority to the high-stakes world of air traffic control to how your voice and presence determine the energy in any room you step into.

If you remember nothing else from this chapter, remember this:

Authority is not about being the loudest—it's about being the clearest.

"People follow confidence, not volume."

Your voice isn't just something people hear, it's something they experience.

Think about the times in your life when you've struggled to command attention. It wasn't because you weren't interesting. And here's the good news: You can change that.

Commanding Attention Is a Choice

Being the whistle isn't about waiting for permission to be heard—it's about owning the moment.

Mr. Horn didn't own the playground because he was the biggest. He owned it because when he blew that whistle, everyone knew exactly what it meant.

That same principle carried over to my days as an air traffic controller. Every pilot I guided outranked me—but inside my airspace, they trusted my voice. They knew exactly who I was and what I represented.

That's exactly who you need to be for every audience you encounter.

Be the voice they recognize.

Be the presence that brings order to chaos.

Be the confidence that reassures them that they're in good hands.

Be the source of joy.

Be the anchor of familiarity.

Be the calm in the middle of the storm.

From this point forward, don't just be another voice in the noise.

Be the whistle.

In the chapters ahead, we will explore strategies to help you not only gain attention but hold it, connect with people in a way that resonates deeply, and leave a lasting impact. Together, we'll learn to cut through the noise and make our presence and content impossible to ignore.

In the chapters ahead, you will learn to **be the whistle.**

Rewind and Reflect Section: Mastering Captivation Key Takeaways

- Commanding attention starts with presence, not volume.

- Confidence and clarity are more powerful than rank or noise.

- One intentional signal can redirect chaos and unify energy.

- Your delivery determines how people experience and respond to your message.

- Being the whistle is about establishing calm, trust, and leadership through tone and timing.

Reflection Questions

- Where in your life do you struggle to hold attention—and why?

- What specific habits weaken your presence or clarity when speaking?

- Who in your life demonstrates whistle-like energy and what can you learn from them?

- How could changing your tone, posture, or phrasing improve how you're received?

- In your current circle or profession, where can you begin to become the whistle?

Action Steps

- Practice commanding attention with a single, authoritative gesture or phrase in your next interaction. Observe the reaction.

- Record yourself giving concise instructions (like an air traffic controller would) and listen back for clarity, speed, and tone.

- Observe leaders (on stage or in meetings), and note how they use energy, timing, and silence to capture a room.

Power Concept

"You don't have to be the loudest. You just have to be the one they trust to lead them through the moment."

CHAPTER 2

Mastering Fear: Audience Decoding

"Mal-Ski, are you ready?" —Stevie Wonder

You've Been Lied To

We've all heard the claim: Public speaking ranks as one of our greatest fears—right up there with death and snakes. We've been flooded with stories of people freezing on stage, blanking out midsentence, or spiraling into panic during presentations, all because they're so afraid. And it's not just myth. Glossophobia, the fear of public speaking, is one of the most common social anxieties, affecting approximately 77% of people to some degree, according to behavioral research.[3] But what if I told you we've been thinking about it all

---

[3] Alexandre Heeren et al., "Assessing Public Speaking Fear with the Short Form of the Personal Report of Confidence as a Speaker Scale: Confirmatory Factor Analyses Among a French-Speaking Community Sample,"
Neuropsychiatric Disease and Treatment 9 (2013): 609–18, https://doi.org/10.2147/NDT.S43097;
T. Furmark et al., "Social Phobia in the General Population: Prevalence and Sociodemographic Profile," *Social Psychiatry and Psychiatric Epidemiology* 34 (1999): 416–24,
https://doi.org/10.1007/s001270050163.

wrong? What if the fear isn't really about speaking at all, but about being fully seen, exposed, and vulnerable in front of a room full of strangers?

Think about it. Talking to people you know is rarely a problem. There's never an issue with rehearsing your presentation for your cat, sibling, or best friend. But the moment you're confronted with unfamiliar faces, everything shifts. Your pulse quickens, your palms sweat, and you start second-guessing every word you've ever learned. Why?

The truth is, our fear isn't rooted in speaking itself—it's in *uncertainty*.

It's the unknown reaction of a roomful of strangers that triggers our most primal survival instinct: ***Avoid rejection***. It's wired into our biology. Back when survival meant staying with the tribe and thriving, rejection could mean life or death. Today, standing on a stage in front of unfamiliar faces may not be life threatening, but our brains haven't fully caught up. To your amygdala—the part of the brain responsible for processing fear—those judgmental stares might as well be saber-toothed tigers.

The kicker is that this fear doesn't limit itself to the stage. It surfaces in every corner of daily life. Ever hesitated to share an idea in a meeting because you weren't sure how the room would react? Avoided asking for a raise because you didn't know if the timing was right? What about that brilliant business pitch you've been sitting on, too afraid to present it to investors? It's the same fear at play—fear of rejection, of judgment, of putting yourself out there without knowing what the response will be. Here's the good news:

That fear can be understood and ultimately mastered.

The secret is to shift your focus. Instead of obsessing over how you'll be received, start paying attention to *who's* receiving you. When you truly understand your audience—be it an auditorium of strangers, a conference room of colleagues, or even your family at the dinner table —you stop performing and start *connecting.*

How to Conquer Fear

Conquering public speaking anxiety isn't about memorizing every word or perfecting your posture—it's about *decoding your audience.* When you truly understand the people you're speaking to—their values, interests, and concerns—you can shape your message so it resonates with what they care about. In that moment, fear loses its grip and is replaced by confidence, because you're no longer bracing for negative reactions. You're inviting collaboration.

This chapter is all about that transformation. We'll explore how to decode an audience's core motivations, anticipate their questions, and craft your message in a way that resonates and connects. By the end, you'll see that fear isn't some unbeatable monster—it's just a puzzle waiting to be solved.

The Stevie Wonder Moment

Picture this: It's a vibrant August evening in downtown Chicago. The air buzzes with excitement as the 2024 Democratic National Convention unfolds. Inside the packed United Center, cameras flash like fireflies. The night is electric as Vice President Kamala Harris prepares to accept the Democratic nomination for president of the United States.

The evening was already a momentous occasion in history, but one of the most anticipated moments was Stevie Wonder's performance. Stevie had agreed to deliver a speech endorsing Kamala, followed by a live performance to inspire voters across the country to rally behind Vice President Harris. I was lucky enough to be accompanying him for this monumental task.

Now, let me be clear: Stevie and I have done shows and tours before. We've worked stages, arenas, and festivals. But this? This was different. The stakes were sky high, as millions of viewers were watching, not just for entertainment but for a moment of unity and possibly a first in history. The weight of that responsibility was enormous.

Backstage, the energy was charged and electric. Celebrities mingled, camera crews adjusted their equipment, and the low hum of anticipation filled the air. The room was alive with the expectation of history being made. The whispers backstage weren't about the politicians or the other celebrities—they were about Stevie. Everyone wanted to see the legend in action.

When Stevie stepped onto the stage, the room transformed. He delivered a short, heartfelt endorsement. His words carried the kind of weight only he could bring, filled with emotion and authenticity. The crowd hung on every syllable. At the conclusion of his speech, Stevie said to the crowd, "I'm depending on you to do, as Spike Lee would say, the right thing." And then, it happened.

Turning slightly toward me, Stevie said, *"Mal-Ski, are you ready?"* The crowd stared. The world watched. And I froze.

I had been prepared to stay out of the limelight, to cue the music from the other side of the stage and keep the energy flowing. But now, with Stevie Wonder calling my name in front of millions, I had no choice but to lean in to it.

For a split second, fear surged through me. My heart raced. My mind scrambled. Was I ready? Had I done enough to rise to this moment?

Then I looked out and saw something I hadn't noticed before: an entire crowd radiating hope. In that moment, it became clear—this wasn't about me at all. It was about them. Every section and every seat was filled with people who had gathered, united by a common belief in a better future. They weren't expecting me to be flawless. They wanted me to harness the energy already pulsing through the room and connect with them on a deeper level. The instant I embraced that perspective, my fear disappeared.

I wasn't just hoping to resonate anymore. I was **amplifying** the collective optimism and channeling it through music and empathy. The event exceeded every expectation I had, leaving me with one undeniable lesson:

When you truly understand your audience, fear has no place.

Reflecting on that breakthrough, I realized that this fear had been with me far longer than I knew—stretching all the way back to junior high.

The Junior High Dance Syndrome

For me, the earliest seeds of that particular kind of fear took root at my first junior high school dance. All my friends had dates they were dancing with, and there I was, nervous, standing on the sidelines, wondering how to ask my crush to dance. Can you remember the feeling? You're standing there, awkward, fearing rejection. Your mind is racing with questions:

- *What if she says no?*

- *What if I embarrass myself in front of everyone?*

I was stuck in place, while my crush stood just a few feet away. I wanted to ask her to dance, but I couldn't muster the courage. My stomach was in knots. I was afraid she'd laugh or walk away, leaving me humiliated in front of my friends.

Looking back, the real problem wasn't my nerves—it was my lack of preparation. I didn't know what my crush liked, what songs made her want to dance, or even if she liked dancing at all. Had I done my research, I would not have been guessing.

Let's imagine for a second I had done my research and decoded my crush. Instead of standing by nervously guessing, hoping, and assuming, I would have known what songs she liked, what dances she could do, and more. I probably would've gone a step further and paid the DJ to play her favorite song by her favorite artist, then quoted her favorite movie while asking her to dance. Can you see how having information brings you confidence and liberates you to be creative in the process? Can you see how the odds of success increase and the nerves decrease when you're armed with information and a plan?

The same principle applies to any audience. If you don't know who you're addressing, you're guessing. But when you've done your homework and decoded your audience, you approach with confidence, not fear.

Think about this in the context of a professional setting. Imagine pitching a product to investors without understanding what they value most. Are they focused on profitability, innovation, or scalability? If you guess, you risk falling flat. But if you've done your homework, you walk in prepared—not to impress them but to connect with them.

That lesson—preparation replacing guesswork—stayed with me. It wasn't just about surviving an awkward middle school moment. It was the foundation for decoding any audience. The principle was simple: When you know your audience, you shift from uncertainty to connection.

But what happens when the stakes are higher? What happens when the audiences aren't just different but dramatically so?

And what if the events happen to be scheduled back-to-back, each demanding a completely unique approach? That's the test I faced one summer—a weekend that would push my ability to decode audiences to its absolute limit.

The Diverse Weekend: From Anxiety to Confidence

One summer, I faced what might be the ultimate audience-decoding challenge: four wildly different events in four days.

- **Friday:** DJing a college pool party on the campus of the University Of Southern California (USC) for over 8,000 students, most of them between 17 and 22 years old. This was a celebration of a new school year for all incoming freshmen and a salute to all the upperclass students for making it this far.

- **Saturday:** Hosting and DJing the NAACP Image Awards celebration along with Doug E. Fresh. This was a celebration of Black excellence, where the cultural elite came together to honor creativity, innovation, and success in the most classy and esteemed way possible.

- **Sunday:** Speaking and teaching at a predominantly African American church in Sacramento, delivering a Bible-based message of hope, purpose, and encouragement to a congregation looking for inspiration and spiritual connection.

- **Monday:** Hosting a school-wide parent-student playdate at my daughter's Montessori school. This involved about 40 kids aged 5–10 with their parents in tow, looking for some fun, energetic, and kid-friendly music and activities.

Let me be honest: The sheer diversity of these events made me nervous. Even after working thousands of events, I still get butterflies when I don't fully understand my audience. And this wasn't just one audience—it was four unique groups.

How do you manage such diversity without losing the audience or your sanity?

One Size Does Not Fit All

As you've probably noticed, there aren't many overlapping strategies for gatherings this varied. Each event needed a unique approach, a custom-fit plan tailored specifically for the crowd I'd be engaging.

Here's what I've learned: The most common mistake speakers, performers, and even leaders make is assuming one size fits all. And let me be clear—***one size does not fit all!***

Take this example: At a New York comedy club, I once saw a comedian who was killing it with a joke about subway rats acting like Walmart greeters. He said, "As you're walking off the train, the rats are standing there with their highlighters, ready to mark your receipt." The whole room erupted with laughter! Why? Because most New Yorkers have experienced subways and—yes—rats. It was relatable.

Then I saw that same comedian at the Laugh Factory in Hollywood, doing the exact same joke. This time? Crickets. No laughter. I even heard someone say, "Ugh, rats are gross." The comedian didn't adjust for his audience—Hollywood doesn't have the subway culture or the same shared experience with rats. That night, he learned the hard way that every audience deserves its own unique approach.

I've seen DJs make the same mistake. Just because a particular song works in Miami doesn't mean it'll work in Los Angeles. Miami nightlife and Los Angeles nightlife couldn't be more different. Each deserves its own decoding and strategy.

Coaches do this too. A play that worked perfectly in last week's game won't necessarily work in this week's game. Team makeup, roster dynamics, and coaching styles can vary wildly. That's why great coaches spend hours watching game film and scouting opponents—they're building a custom plan for each specific matchup.

So, for my diverse weekend, I knew I needed four completely different custom approaches. And let me tell you, the nerves were real.

Friday: USC Pool Party

For the USC pool party, I reached out to the main fraternities and sororities I knew would be at the party. I asked what some of their favorite songs were and which artists I would be surprised that they all loved. They gave me a list of songs they strolled to and pointed me to a USC artist who'd released a SoundCloud track that had become a campus anthem. Jackpot. I built my setlist around that vibe, including local hits and crowd favorites, and walked into the party prepared to make it feel like their own personal celebration.

The energy was electric. Students danced as if there were no tomorrow, singing along to songs they knew and loved. The moment that I played that USC anthem? Wow! The crowd lost it. It wasn't just music—it was a connection to their culture, their experiences, and their pride. One random student actually told me afterward that I had played all of her favorite songs from her personal playlist. Mission accomplished.

Saturday: NAACP Image Awards

The NAACP Image Awards required a completely different approach. This wasn't a wild party— it was a sophisticated celebration of Black excellence. The stakes were high, and I knew the audience expected elegance, respect, and cultural relevance.

I started by talking to the NAACP chair and Doug E. Fresh himself to understand the evening's vision. I also reached out to a few nominees to get a sense of their expectations and favorite songs. This wasn't about playing what was trending—it was about curating a soundtrack that honored the history and legacy of the moment.

When the event began, the room felt as if it were on fire, not from wild energy but from the pride and unity that filled the air. Every choice I made that night, from crowd engagement to performing alongside the "World's Greatest Entertainer," Doug E. Fresh, reflected the excellence we were there to celebrate.

Sunday: Sacramento Church Service

On Sunday, I switched gears again, stepping into the role of a speaker. This wasn't about DJing. It was about delivering a biblically based message of hope and purpose to a congregation looking for spiritual nourishment.

I spent hours in conversation with the senior pastor, diving into the church's values and previous messages. I also researched their Facebook page to get a sense of the congregation's demographics and what mattered most to them.

When I stepped up to speak, I wasn't just delivering words—I was connecting directly to the hearts of people I felt I now knew. The feedback after the service confirmed what I'd hoped:

The message had landed exactly where it needed to.

Monday: Montessori Playdate

Finally, on Monday, I stepped into an entirely different world: a school playdate with kids and parents. Here, the focus wasn't on history, legacy, or spiritual growth—it was on fun, joy, and connection.

To prepare, I tapped into my secret weapon: my daughter. I asked her about her classmates' favorite songs, shows, and activities, and I cross-referenced that with input from other parents. Armed with that intel, I planned activities that kept the kids laughing and moving —and, to my surprise, got the parents just as involved.

One highlight I'll never forget: a spontaneous dance-off between the kids and their parents. The room was full of laughter, cheers, and pure joy.

The Takeaway

Each event went incredibly well. The USC students danced all night. The NAACP crowd celebrated in unity. The church congregation connected with my message and left inspired. And the kids? They had a blast—but I think the parents may have enjoyed it even more.

What started with fear turned into one of the most rewarding weekends of my career.

Cultural Nuances: Speaking Their Language

Every audience has its own culture—a shared set of values, experiences, and traditions that shape how they connect. This culture influences not just what the audience finds relatable but also how they perceive authenticity, humor, and even authority. Ignoring these nuances is like trying to have a meaningful conversation in a language you don't speak—it creates disconnect instead of resonance. If you truly want to engage and captivate, you have to step into the audience's world, understand their unspoken rules, and speak in a way that says, "I see you. I respect you. I'm one of you."

Connecting with your audience on this level requires more than surface-level preparation. It's about digging deeper to understand the intricacies of their world—their struggles, their aspirations, and the unique quirks that make them who they are. Every culture has its own rhythm, its own inside jokes, and its own way of looking at the world. Your job as a speaker, performer, or leader is to tune into that rhythm and use it to build a bridge of trust and familiarity.

Chicago Bears Versus Green Bay Packers = Passion

Imagine this: You're asked to speak to a room full of die-hard Chicago Bears fans. If you've done your homework and decoded your audience, you'll know that their rivalry with the Green Bay Packers isn't just a sports feud—it's practically a cultural religion. Armed with that knowledge, you could crack a well-timed joke about the Packers and immediately win over the room. Why? Because you've shown them that you "get it." You've spoken their language, and in doing so, you've earned their trust and attention.

Culture Is the Code

Cultural nuances go far beyond sports rivalries or regional quirks. They're embedded in the way people dress, the music they listen to, the slang they use, and even the food they eat. For instance, if you're addressing a group of *Sneaker-heads*, you understand that they are deeply immersed in sneaker culture. In turn, you wouldn't show up in dress shoes—you'd lace up a fresh pair of Air Jordans or classic Nike Dunks. If you really wanted to make an impression, you would research an extremely hard-to-find pair of retros that would make a scene. From the second you walked in, you would have instant credibility. That simple, intentional choice would communicate volumes before you even opened your mouth. It's not just about looking the part— it's about showing that you've taken the time to understand their world.

The same principle applies whether you're addressing a room full of tech entrepreneurs, a congregation at a church, or a group of middle school students. Each audience has its own unwritten rules, and when you take the time to learn them, you're not just speaking to them— you're connecting with them.

Think of cultural nuances as a secret handshake. It's an unspoken agreement that says, "I see you. I value you. I'm not here to impose my world on yours—I'm here to meet you where you are." When you speak someone's language, whether literally or metaphorically, you create an immediate bond of trust and familiarity. And trust? That's the foundation of every great performance, presentation, and interaction.

Warning: Don't Skip the Homework

Here's the part most people miss: **Cultural nuance isn't something you can fake.** If you try to adopt the slang, style, or humor of a culture without truly understanding it, you risk coming across as inauthentic—or worse, disrespectful. That's why doing your homework isn't optional— it's essential.

Listen, observe, and learn before you speak.

Pay attention to the little details that make a big difference.

And most importantly, approach every audience with empathy and a genuine desire to connect, not just perform.

Because when people feel as if you've taken the time to understand their world, they're not just more open to what you have to say—they're more likely to remember it. And that's the ultimate goal, isn't it? To create a connection so strong, an impression so lasting, that your message lingers long after the moment has passed.

Confidence Through Clarity

At every stage—whether it was standing beside Stevie Wonder in front of millions, navigating a pool party of college freshmen, or speaking hope to a congregation—one truth remained: confidence follows clarity. The more I understood who I was speaking to, the less room fear had to speak back. That's the key. You don't silence fear by trying to be perfect—you silence fear by being prepared, present, and people-focused. Know your audience, and fear loses its grip.

Rewind and Reflect Section: Mastering Fear Key

Takeaways

- Fear of public speaking is often rooted in uncertainty—not speaking itself.

- Understanding your audience reduces anxiety and builds authentic connection.

- Connection replaces performance when you focus on who's receiving your message.

- Preparation and empathy are key to transforming fear into confidence.

- Audience decoding is a strategic tool, not just a soft skill. It empowers delivery.

Reflection Questions

- What situations trigger your fear of speaking or performing in front of others?

- When have you felt most confident on stage or in front of a group—and why?

- How well do you currently prepare for the specific needs of your audience? - What could you do differently to study or learn about your next audience? - How does understanding your audience give you an advantage in everyday communication?

Action Steps

- Before your next presentation, interview, or performance, identify three things your audience values or struggles with.

- Reframe nerves as preparation energy: Tell yourself, "I'm not nervous, I'm getting ready."

- Apply audience decoding in a casual setting—notice how people respond when you reflect their values and language.

Power Concept

"When you truly understand your audience, fear has no place."

Chapter 3

Mastering First Impressions: Crafting Hellos

"Everyone, please welcome to the stage..."
"Good morning, class. I'd like you to meet..."

Crafting Hellos

It's within the first few seconds that everything matters most. This is where it all hangs in the balance. Regardless of the setting—a formal stage, a classroom, or simply a first-time introduction—the initial moments set the tone for everything that follows. Yes, you're there to connect, provide value, and deliver what your audience wants and needs. But it's during these fleeting first seconds that you determine just how easy—or challenging—that journey will be. What truly defines a first impression? In her book *Presence*, social psychologist Amy Cuddy explains that within seconds of meeting someone, people assess two key things:

1. "Can I trust this person?"

2. "Can I respect this person?"[4]

Let's break these down. When people ask themselves "Can I trust this person?," they're gauging whether you feel safe, relatable, and authentic. Trust is foundational in any relationship, personal or professional. If your audience doesn't trust you—if they sense even a hint of insincerity—it doesn't matter how brilliant your message is. Trust makes people lean in. It opens the door for real connection. Think about a speaker you've admired. Was it their credentials that hooked you first, or was it the way they made you feel seen and heard?

The second question, "Can I respect this person?," is about competence and credibility. Once trust is established, respect assures your audience that you have the expertise or authority to back up what you're saying. People need to feel that you're knowledgeable and capable enough to lead them on the journey you're about to take together.

So, how much of our lives is driven by these two factors—trust and respect? The answer is nearly everything. From our personal relationships to our career decisions, we instinctively lean toward people and organizations we both trust and respect. Think about your closest friendships, your favorite mentors, or

---

4 Cuddy, *Presence*, 94.

even your go-to brands. Each of them likely earned your trust and respect at some point, creating a foundation for that bond.

As Malcolm Gladwell perfectly explains in his book *Blink*, sometimes we can know more about someone or something in the blink of an eye than we can after months of study.[5]

"Ugh" at First Sight

Yet, as crucial as those opening seconds are for establishing trust and respect, they can also go wrong—leading to what I call "'Ugh' at first sight," a misstep so potent that it overshadows everything else you hoped to accomplish. Unfortunately, I've seen this firsthand.

In my freshman year of college, my two best friends dated two sisters. These sisters had an older sister whom my best friends were eager for me to connect with. I'd heard she was very successful and attractive, and my friends were excited about setting us up. So, we all planned to meet at a restaurant so she and I could get acquainted.

I arrived a little early, and instead of heading straight to the table, I wanted to wash my hands and make sure my outfit

---

[5] Malcolm Gladwell, *Blink: The Power of Thinking Without Thinking* (Back Bay Books, 2005), paraphrase.

was right. As I was washing up, I overheard a woman right outside the restroom in the hallway on the phone.

This woman was really going off—cursing like I'd never heard before, using every foul word you can imagine, all directed at some guy on the phone. All I could think about was how unattractive it was for people to talk like that, and how I couldn't imagine being with someone who spoke to me that way.

I finished washing my hands and headed to the table. I greeted my friends with a fist bump, said hello to their girlfriends, and jokingly asked the sisters, "Where's your sister? Let me guess, she got cold feet?"

They said, "She went to the restroom. She'll be back in a second."

And I thought, "Oh no, please don't let it be the woman I overheard."

Just then, the sisters began to stand and smile, and as I turned around, it was her—the same woman I had overheard. She walked up, smiling and trying to be bubbly and nice. "Hi, Jamal! It's so nice to finally meet you. I've heard so many great things about you." I couldn't even pay attention to how she was greeting me—all I could think about were the words I had overheard her saying to that guy on the phone.

For the entire dinner, I didn't believe anything she said. Every compliment she gave, I doubted its authenticity. Every fact she stated, I questioned. She was very successful as I'd been told and educated too, but that initial encounter had overshadowed it all. Also, she was very attractive—a beautiful woman—but my first impression of her had tainted even the way I saw her beauty.

The point is that sometimes, any attraction, potential value, or significance in content— all of it can be overshadowed and tainted by a terrible first impression.

Those initial moments don't just determine how people perceive you—they set the tone for whether they're willing to engage with you at all.

GirlsBuild LA

There was one particular time I had to apply the importance of first impressions in real time—at GirlsBuild LA.

This event, organized by the LA Promise Fund, took place at the Los Angeles Convention Center. They bused in 8,000 young girls from the LA Unified School District for a half-day event filled with panels, interviews, and speeches from incredibly inspiring and successful women from around the world, including influential figures like Ibtihaj Muhammad, Kamala Harris, and Hillary Clinton. My role was both DJ and host, curating the overall energy of the discussions, panels, and interviews. My task was to ensure the energy remained high and positive throughout the entire day.

As you can imagine, at an event like GirlsBuild LA, being the only male host and curator can be a fragile task. With that in mind, my first impression had to be on point. It had to be intentional and meaningful because I was the only nonfemale to grace that stage. I would be the only example outside of the female circle for the entire event, so my approach had to speak volumes.

The time came for me to be introduced. When I walked on stage, the first thing anyone saw was my Candace Parker jersey beneath my jacket. If you know anything about me, then you know how much I love and admire WNBA legend Candace Parker. She embodies greatness, authenticity and all the characteristics of a champion. So I wore her jersey with pride. I pointed to it as I came on stage, and I heard some of the girls start to chant, "MVP! MVP!" I opened my jacket to draw more attention to it, and the chants grew louder across the room.

Reaching the microphone, the first thing I said was, "Wow, you all look amazing. I wish my two daughters could see how strong, intelligent, and incredible the girls of the LA Unified School District are. Are you girls ready to take over the world?"

And they screamed, "Yeah!"

"Are you ready to take over the world?"

"Yeah!"

"Well, let's get to it!"

To set the tone, I kicked off with one of the biggest trending songs among their age group. I had done my research (decoded the audience) by asking two of my high school–age nieces what they were into. This enabled me to identify the trending songs, quotes, and slang that only high school girls were using at that time. By speaking their language, I was able to validate their culture as teenage girls and let them know that I stood with them for the empowerment of all women.

The reason I mentioned my daughters was to underscore the fact that I'm a girl dad and absolutely stand for the upliftment of all women. Every day, I am surrounded by amazing women — my wife and my daughters—all of whom make me better. I wanted these young girls to feel that and know my alignment and commitment to women's empowerment from the very first impression.

Moments like these underscore the tremendous impact a first impression can make. Whether your own first impression is during a chance meeting in a restaurant or a high-profile event like GirlsBuild LA, your initial moments in front of an audience can either pave the way for connection or shut it down. But these aren't just one-off lucky breaks or disastrous missteps —they're results you can *intentionally* guide. So, how do you make sure your own introductions always hit the mark? The good news is, there's a method to mastering these pivotal seconds, and that's exactly what we'll explore next.

How to Effectively Master First Impressions

Making a strong first impression isn't about luck or chance—it's about intentionality.

The good news? There are practical steps you can take to ensure that those first critical seconds leave a lasting impact. Here are four key areas to focus on to do it effectively.

1. Dress the Part

Your attire speaks louder than your first words. Before people hear what you have to say, they'll see you—and what you're wearing will immediately influence their perception of you. How you dress can inspire confidence, show respect, and create instant rapport. Dressing well signals that you've taken the time to think about your audience. It's a way of saying, "I see you, and I respect this moment we're about to share."

In chapter 2, we talked about decoding your audience—studying their values, culture, and expectations. The same principles apply to your wardrobe. When you understand your audience, you can tailor your outfit to enhance your message while creating a connection.

For example, think about that wild weekend with the diverse events that I talked about in chapter 2. Deciding what to wear for each audience wasn't easy—it gave me more anxiety than the content I was preparing to deliver did! That's why I consulted with my team of trendy stylists to figure out the best outfits for each event. Each wardrobe choice was intentional, ensuring I aligned with the expectations of the crowd.

But let's be clear: Dressing is not one size fits all. Imagine if I had walked into the church service wearing the same shorts and USC tank top I wore to the pool party. The congregation would have been appalled. Or what if I had shown up at my daughter's school playdate in a formal suit and tie? Those kids wouldn't have taken me seriously for a second.

Now, flip it. Picture showing up to a formal gala in jeans and sneakers. Even if you deliver the most compelling message of your life, that initial disconnect in appearance will stick. Dressing intentionally isn't about impressing people—it's about respecting their expectations and showing them you understand their world.

2. Consider Visual Impact and Body Language

Your body language and visual cues play a huge role in how you're perceived. According to studies by psychologist Albert Mehrabian, 87% of communication is nonverbal. Mehrabian's research found that when it comes to conveying feelings and attitudes, 93% of the emotional impact comes from nonverbal elements—38% from tone and 55% from facial expressions.[6] That means your gestures, posture, and even facial expressions are conveying more than your words or content—whether you realize it or not.

At the GirlsBuild LA event, my Candace Parker jersey did the talking before I even picked up the mic. The audience didn't just see a jersey—they saw someone who understood and aligned with their excitement and values. Candace had just won a WNBA championship at the Crypto.com Arena next door, and I knew that wearing her jersey would tap into the pride these young women already felt.

Beyond clothing, your body language must project confidence and connection. Stand tall, maintain eye contact, and use open gestures. These simple nonverbal cues can immediately establish trust and make your audience feel at ease.

---

[6] Albert Mehrabian, *Silent Messages* (Wadsworth Publishing Company, 1971), 43.

Let's not forget the importance of a smile. A warm, genuine smile says, "I'm approachable, I'm here for you, and I'm excited about this moment." Never underestimate the power of a smile to disarm even the most skeptical crowd.

3. Have a Clear Purpose

After your appearance and body language have done their work, the next step is clarity. Your audience needs to know, from the outset, why you're there and what they can expect. This doesn't mean launching into every detail of your presentation—it means giving your audience a road map for the journey you're about to take together.

For example, at the GirlsBuild LA event, I started with a simple but powerful question: "Are you girls ready to take over the world?" That one line set the tone for the entire day. It was clear, empowering, and directly aligned with the event's purpose of inspiring young girls to lead and succeed.

Clarity isn't just about words—it's about creating a moment of shared understanding. When people know what's coming, they feel more comfortable and open to engaging with your message.

4. Make an Emotional Connection

Emotional connection is the glue that makes your first impression stick. It's what turns a good moment into a memorable one. The key to creating a connection is to show vulnerability and authenticity. People are drawn to those who aren't afraid to share pieces of themselves—those who make their audiences feel something. That emotional spark is what transforms a fleeting introduction into a lasting impact.

Think about the performances, speeches, or interactions that have stayed with you. Were they the most polished? Maybe not. But they were real. They touched your heart, made you laugh, or gave you hope. That's the magic of emotional connection—it transcends words and leaves a mark on the soul.

At the GirlsBuild LA event, I shared how my daughters inspire me to stand for women's empowerment. That wasn't just a line I threw in for applause—it was a genuine expression of my values, and it resonated with the audience. When I said, "I wish my two daughters could see how strong, intelligent, and incredible the girls of the LA Unified School District are," I could see nods and smiles ripple across the crowd. It wasn't just about me anymore. It was about us. It created a shared emotional experience that elevated the energy in the room.

Here's the thing about emotion—it lingers. Long after people forget your words, they'll remember how you made them feel. Did you leave them inspired? Encouraged? Challenged? Your ability to evoke emotion determines how deeply your first impression will resonate.

First Impressions That Stick

Think back to your earliest days in school. Maybe there's a friend—or even a former classmate —you still refer to by a nickname you gave them based on your first impression of them. You laugh now as you reflect on how they got that nickname. It was a single first impression that they are now identified by. That's how powerful those initial encounters can be.

I'll never forget my own ninth-grade crush, who to this day calls me "Giggles." I earned that nickname because the very first time we met, I was so overwhelmed by her beauty that I could barely form a sentence. Instead, I giggled at almost every-thing she said—nervously smiling and laughing without pause. It was an unintentional display of my nerves and excitement, and she's never let me forget it. In that split second, I created an im-pression that has lasted over a decade.

Now, let's flip the script. Imagine using that same power to create a life-changing experience for someone else. What if, years from now, a person looks back on your very first meeting as the moment they decided to take a risk, invest in themselves, or follow a big dream— because of something you said or simply how you made them feel? That's the true potential of a first impression.

It's not just about superficial pleasantries or lighthearted banter. A well-crafted, intentional hello can lay the foundation for lasting trust, mutual respect, and genuine connection. Whether you're meeting a potential mentor or client, introducing yourself to a new team, or speaking at a major event, the way you show up in those opening moments can shift the course of a conversation, a deal, or even a career path.

The power of first impressions doesn't lie in being perfect—it lies in being *intentional.* By choosing how you appear, what you say, and how you say it, you can convey authenticity, respect, and openness. You can spark curiosity and invite people to see the best in you—just as you want to see the best in them. And the effects of that initial moment can reverberate far beyond the situation at hand, influencing how others speak about you, remember you, and decide to collaborate with you in the future.

Control Your Hello

Every day, we're presented with opportunities to make first impressions. Whether it's introducing yourself in a meeting, walking into a room of strangers, or simply greeting someone new, those first few moments can shape how people see you—and how much they're willing to trust and respect you.

Think about it. How many times have you judged someone based on their first impression? How many times have you replayed an introduction in your mind, wishing you could do it over? The truth is, we all know what it feels like to get it right—and what it feels like to miss the mark.

But here's the good news: You don't have to leave your first impressions to chance. You can take control. You can dress intentionally, set the tone with your body language, be clear about your purpose, and connect emotionally with those around you. These aren't just tools for the stage or the spotlight—they're skills for life, tools that empower you to show up as your best self in every interaction.

So, the next time you meet someone—whether it's in a meeting, on a stage, or even in passing—take a moment to consider the story you're about to tell through your presence, your words, and your actions. Think about the message you want to send and how it aligns with who you truly are.

Ask yourself the following:

- Am I presenting myself in a way that reflects my values and intentions?

- Am I using every tool I have—my appearance, my body language, my tone—to create a positive and memorable impression?

- Am I crafting a hello that will leave people eager to know more?

Your hello is more than a greeting. It's your opportunity to establish trust and respect, to build a connection that opens doors, and to set the tone for the journey ahead. When you show up with intentionality and authenticity, you don't just make an impression—you create an opportunity for engagement, trust, and lasting impact.

But don't overthink it. The beauty of mastering first impressions isn't about being perfect —it's about being present. It's about showing up as your best self and letting that shine through in a way that others can see, feel, and connect with.

So, as you walk into your next introduction, *craft your hello*.

Let it be bold. Let it be thoughtful. Let it be you.

Crafting hellos is how you master the art of the first impression. You're not just starting a conversation—you're setting the stage for something far greater.

You're establishing a connection. You're **mastering the crowd.**

Rewind and Reflect Section: Mastering First Impressions

Key Takeaways

- First impressions shape trust and respect within seconds of any interaction.

- Visual cues, tone, and body language carry more weight than words alone.

- Intention and emotional connection are vital to establishing credibility early.

- Your hello sets the tone for everything that follows, so control it with purpose.

- Cultural awareness and personal authenticity create a lasting first impression.

Reflection Questions

- What do people typically notice about you first—and is it intentional?

- How can you adjust your appearance or body language to better match your message?

- When have you made a first impression you're proud of—and what made it effective?

- What assumptions might people make about you based on your introduction?

- How could you create a more powerful, authentic introduction in future settings?

Action Steps

- Practice delivering your self-introduction to a mirror or friend. Focus on tone, eye contact, and clarity.

- Before your next interaction, choose your outfit, posture, and tone intentionally based on your audience.

- Write and rehearse a 15-second elevator pitch that immediately reflects trust and respect.

Power Concept

Crafting hellos means being intentional about the first impression you make—knowing that long before you speak, you're already telling a story.

Chapter 4

Mastering Subtle Rebellion: Rebels with a Cause

"I'm probably going to get in trouble for saying this…"
"They asked me not to say this but it's too important for me not to share…"

The Allure

What is it about statements like these that make us all lean in, that make our ears perk up? Is it the enticement of the forbidden—clickbait for our ears, drawing us in with irresistible intrigue? Could it be the allure of being privy to exclusive insider information? Or is it that each of us has a rebel deep down inside us, waiting for another rebel to inspire us to rise up and challenge some status quo?

The answer is all of the above. Yes, yes, and yes.

For years, I've studied crowd psychology. I've DJed and hosted thousands of events, engaging with every kind of demographic imaginable. From inner-city neighborhoods to hillside mansions, roaring sports stadiums to backyard bar mitzvahs, country music festivals to EDM raves, hip-hop clubs to lively Kidz Bop parties, I've seen it all. I've stood alongside legendary artists commanding millions of fans, as well as first-time performers nervously stepping onto local stages. I've delivered keynotes at massive conferences and taught intimate Sunday school lessons to teenagers. Across all these settings, I've learned one universal concept that has worked in every context: subtle rebellion.

(Subtle rebellion: the art of gently bending, teasing, or inventing "rules" and then breaking them in a way that entices your audience to lean in and possibly react)

The power of gently breaking expectations transcends every type of audience, uniting them in a shared moment of curiosity, excitement, and intrigue. But I didn't truly grasp the power of subtle rebellion until I found myself caught up in it.

The Power of Subtle Rebellion

I was visiting a church near Pasadena, California. It was an affluent congregation with about 400 people in attendance, a beautifully diverse mix of races and generations. The pastor, a friend of mine, was mid-sermon when he noticed some teenagers talking, laughing, and giggling in the section behind mine. Since he hadn't said anything funny, I assumed he felt as if he was losing their attention.

Abruptly, he stopped mid-thought and said, "Can I just be transparent for a second?" (even though he'd already been extremely honest so far). He continued, "I know I'm probably going to get in trouble for saying this, and I'm sure I'll get tons of emails about what I'm about to say. I know the church mothers and staff would never approve of me saying this, but…"

(Pause.)

He hadn't even said what it was yet, but I was already on the edge of my seat, eager to capture whatever rebellious idea was coming next. It was like waiting for the big twist in a suspense movie. His setup was so powerful that it had me hooked before he'd even delivered the punch line.

I also noticed that right after he said this, all the talking stopped. The giggles halted. Dead silence. The anticipation was loud.

After a very pregnant pause, he finally said, "I *love* this new Kendrick Lamar song. I know I'm not supposed to love it, but I do!"

He went on to describe how Kendrick had united the country against one of the biggest Canadian rappers at the time, dissecting the message behind the song Not Like Us. He then pivoted back to his sermon, comparing Kendrick's boldness to the idea that God called us to stand out, just as K-Dot did. He tied it into the concept that those living outside the boundaries of a faith-led life, trying to colonize God's culture for profit, should be called out and stood against in the same way.

By this point, *he had me.* I was glued. The teenagers who had been uninterested before? Now they were on the edges of their seats, engaged! The skeptical mothers in the front row? Intrigued and connected.

Had he started off with "God's culture is being colonized," I might not have even paid attention. But the way he set it up— by framing it as a rebellious confession—captivated the room. It made his message resonate with every single person there.

Activating Reactance

At the heart of our fascination with rebellion lies a psychological principle called "**reactance**." Reactance is the emotional and cognitive response we experience when we feel our freedoms or choices are restricted or threatened. When people sense their independence being limited, they instinctively push back—often by doing the very thing they've been told not to do.[7]

This is why phrases like "I'm probably going to get in trouble for saying this" or "You're not supposed to know this" are so powerful. They don't just hint at forbidden knowledge—they challenge the audience's sense of freedom. It's not just about the allure of breaking the rules. It's about our deeply ingrained need to defend our autonomy.

Imagine being told not to peek at a Christmas gift hidden in the closet. The moment you hear "don't," your curiosity intensifies. The box sitting in the closet becomes a magnet for your attention, not because of what's inside but because you've been told you can't open it. That's reactance in action. It's an emotional response that demands we reclaim the choice that feels restricted, even if it's over something trivial.

Reactance is hardwired into us. When we're children, being told "Don't touch that" or "Don't say that" ignites a desire to do exactly the opposite. This principle follows us into adulthood,

---

[7] Jack Williams Brehm, *A Theory of Psychological Reactance* (Academic Press, 1966); James Price Dillard and Lijang Shen, "On the Nature of Reactance and Its Role in Persuasive Health Communication," *Communication Monographs* 72, no. 2 (2005): 144–68, https://doi.org/10.1080/03637750500111815; Claude Miller et al., "Psychological Reactance and Promotional Health Messages: The Effects of Controlling Language, Lexical Concreteness, and the Restoration of Freedom," *Human Communication Research* 33, no. 2 (2007): 219–40, https://doi.org/10.1111/j.1468-2958.2007.00297.x.

influencing everything from the choices we make to the media we consume.

Subtle rebellion leverages this instinct. By teasing rules, bending expectations, or hinting at exclusivity, you engage the audience's innate drive to assert their freedom. When a pastor says, "I'm probably going to get in trouble for saying this," or a brand markets something as "what *they* don't want you to know," they trigger this exact response, creating intrigue and inspiring action.

Steve Jobs and the "Think Different" Campaign

Few brands have embraced subtle rebellion more effectively than Apple under Steve Jobs. In the late 1990s, Apple was struggling, and Jobs's bold solution was to launch the now-iconic "Think

Different" campaign. This concept was a love letter to the "misfits," "rebels," and

"troublemakers" who dared to defy conventional wisdom. The campaign's unforgettable slogan, "Think Different," wasn't a direct attack on the status quo—it was an invitation to *not be limited* by it. Apple didn't tell people to break rules outright. Instead, it nudged them to reimagine what was possible by simply *thinking* in a way others weren't.

In essence, Jobs crafted an environment where reactance could thrive. By praising "the crazy ones…who see things differently,"[8] Jobs's Apple teased a forbidden idea: that it's not just okay to question norms and limitations—it's admirable. The ads featured people like Albert Einstein, Mahatma Gandhi, and Amelia Earhart, all figures who had collectively rewritten society's rules. By framing these icons as kindred spirits of Apple's audience, Jobs played to our desire for autonomy, creativity, and boundary pushing. He never said, "You must rebel." He just hinted that to do otherwise was to miss your chance to be extraordinary.

The impact? Consumers leaned in. They felt they were part of a movement, not just purchasing another gadget. They were *coconspirators* in Apple's mission to stand out. To this day, Apple continues to harness this spirit of subtle rebellion. Even its product launches feel less like corporate announcements and more like unveiling secrets the world isn't supposed to know yet. This perpetuates a sense of excitement, exclusivity, and quiet challenge to the status quo— hallmarks of reactance done right.

Next time you see an Apple keynote or recall the famous "Crazy Ones" ads, notice how the brand never overtly demands that you rebel. Instead, it invites you into a narrative that suggests that greatness is found by those who dare to step outside the

---

[8] Apple, "Crazy Ones" television advertisement, TBWA\Chiat\Day, directed by Jennifer Golub, 1997.

boundaries of the ordinary. That gentle nudge is precisely the art of subtle rebellion. It doesn't force you to join but rather sparks the desire within you to break free from whatever box you feel society has placed you in, all while feeling as if you made the choice yourself. Brilliant.

Breaking the Rules We Made

Sometimes, the most powerful rules to break are the ones we created in the first place. The key to subtle rebellion isn't about defying authority outright. It's about crafting the illusion of a boundary just so you can shatter it. When an expectation is set, people instinctively lean in, waiting to see if it will be upheld or challenged. And when that expectation is flipped on its head, it sparks a rush of energy and engagement and even a sense of collective defiance.

Nowhere is this more evident than in one of my favorite moments from the LA Memorial Coliseum. As the official DJ for the USC Trojans football team, I've been a part of countless incredible moments, but one stands out.

It was a beautiful afternoon in downtown Los Angeles. The USC Trojans were facing Nebraska, and although the stadium was packed with about 60,000 fans, the energy wasn't quite where it needed to be. Our in-game show caller and producer,

Daniel Zerunyan, had a brilliant idea to shift the momentum in the fourth quarter.

On the digital boards that everyone could see, he posted:

"Warning: Nebraska has requested that we remain silent when they're on offense."

It wasn't true, of course. Nebraska hadn't made any such request. But the moment it appeared, it created a perceived boundary. So, I grabbed the mic and leaned into it:

"USC family, Nebraska has requested that we remain silent when they're on offense.

What do you say to that?"

The crowd erupted. What started as a moderate roar turned into a deafening wall of sound. The stadium was electrified. USC ended up scoring in the fourth quarter, taking the lead and winning the game.

The genius of this move wasn't just that it engaged the audience—it was that we had created the "rule" ourselves. By inventing a restriction and then encouraging the crowd to defy it, we tapped into their reactance. They weren't just cheering for their team—they were rebelling against the idea that someone else could control their actions. If you know college students and you know college football fans, then you know this idea was just the right spark needed to ignite our crowd's fire. This moment didn't just energize the audience—it united them. Together, they pushed back against a fabricated limitation, proving that sometimes the most powerful rules to break are the ones you create.

Parenting with Subtle Rebellion

Parents have long been masters of applying the art of subtle rebellion to create unforgettable moments. If you've ever been around kids, you know they love breaking the rules—just not the ones that get them grounded. It's the small, controlled acts of defiance that spark their joy. As parents, we can use that instinct to our advantage.

Think about how many times a parent says, **"I know we normally eat breakfast in the morning, but let's shake things up—let's have pancakes for dinner!"** That tiny act of breaking routine transforms an ordinary meal into a mini adventure. Suddenly, the same pancakes that kids might normally complain about feel like the most exciting dinner they've ever had. Nothing about the food has changed—just the framing of the experience.

Or consider the times parents surprise their kids with ice cream before dinner, turn a school night into an impromptu movie marathon, or let the kids jump on the bed even though the house rules say otherwise. These moments of playful rebellion make kids feel special. They feel like they're in on something—like they've won a little victory against the *boring* rules of everyday life. That feeling of being part of something exclusive? That's exactly what makes it stick in their memory forever.

Want proof that subtle rebellion works? Just think about the moments from your own childhood that stand out the most. Chances are, some of your favorite memories aren't the ones where everything went according to plan—they're the ones where someone broke the script in the best way possible. The time a teacher threw out the lesson plan and let the class have a discussion about something that truly mattered to them. The time your parents let you stay up late to watch a movie *just this once*. The time you and your friends dared to bend a rule and got away with it.

That's the magic of subtle rebellion. It doesn't just make moments *fun*—it makes them *memorable*. When used intentionally, it becomes one of the most powerful tools for connection, influence, and engagement.

The Mechanics of Subtle Rebellion

Subtle rebellion isn't about outright defiance—it's about strategic disruption. It's about bending the rules just enough to create intrigue, but not so much that you lose credibility. It's about knowing exactly when to break the script, flip the expectation, or tease the forbidden in a way that makes people lean in instead of tuning out.

The key to making it work? Control.

The best moments of subtle rebellion don't come from chaos. They come from wellplaced, intentional moments where you guide your audience into a space of curiosity, anticipation, and engagement. It's a balance—push too hard, and you risk alienation. Play it too safe, and you'll never capture their attention in the first place.

So how do you pull it off? It comes down to **four essential steps.**

1. Tease the Forbidden

Few things capture attention like the *hint* of something we're not supposed to hear.

When you set up an idea with phrases like "I probably shouldn't say this, but…," "I know I'm going to get in trouble for this, but you need to hear it…," or "I was told to stick to the script, but I just can't…," you immediately activate curiosity. Your audience instinctively leans in because now they *have to* know what you're about to say.

Why? **Because our brains are wired to crave exclusivity.** The moment you suggest that something is off limits, it becomes *more* valuable. We've seen this tactic used everywhere—from marketing campaigns ("What they don't want you to know!") to movie trailers ("The scene they tried to cut!") to everyday conversations ("I shouldn't tell you this, but…"). It works because it makes people feel like insiders.

Want proof? Try it in casual conversation. The next time you're with a group of people, lower your voice slightly and say, "Okay, this has to stay between us…" and watch how quickly they stop what they're doing to listen. That's the power of teasing the forbidden.

2. Build Suspense

Suspense is the fuel that drives engagement. If you tease something forbidden but immediately reveal it, you lose the magic. The secret is in the **pause**—the space between curiosity and payoff.

Great storytellers, comedians, and speakers all understand this. They don't rush through their punchlines—they let the audience sit in anticipation, savoring the moment before the reveal.

Think about a magician about to reveal a trick. If they snap their fingers too quickly, the effect is gone. But if they pause—if they let the tension build—*that's* when the audience is locked in.

In communication, that pause works the same way. If you say, "Okay, this is off the record..."

[Pause, let them lean in, and let them wait.]

"This generation hears more truth in rap lyrics than in most pulpits."

The pause amplifies the impact. It makes the reveal feel *bigger*, even if the statement itself isn't earth shattering.

Try this: Next time you have an important message to deliver, don't rush it. Give your audience space to anticipate. Let them *need* to hear what you have to say next.

3. Deliver the Content—and Make It Worth It

If you've built suspense but don't have a strong reveal, you've wasted the setup. You can't hint at something groundbreaking and then deliver something underwhelming.

Your rebellion—your break from the norm—has to matter.

Think about that pastor in Pasadena who paused before revealing his love for a Kendrick Lamar song. It worked because his statement had *real* weight. He didn't just say it for shock value—he tied it into a message that resonated. It had meaning.

So when you reach this step, ask yourself: "What's the real takeaway?"

If you're teasing an unpopular opinion, does it challenge the audience to think differently? If you're breaking a rule, does it actually elevate the moment? If you're disrupting the norm, does it add value to the experience? *Rebellion for rebellion's sake isn't engaging.*

4. Create Rules Just to Break Them

One of the best ways to create engagement? Invent a rule—then break it.

We saw this in action at that **USC versus Nebraska** football game when we put that message on the big screen: "Nebraska has requested that we remain silent when they're on offense."

Again, it wasn't true. Nebraska never made that request. But the moment fans read it, they collectively thought, "Oh, absolutely not."

And just like that, the entire stadium erupted into a deafening noise.

Why did it work? Because people love to rebel against standards and limitations— especially when they feel like they're reclaiming control.

But beyond just activating rebellion, breaking a rule can also make people feel valued. When they see that you're willing to bend or break a rule for *them*, it makes them feel as if they matter.

I once saw a famous motivational speaker use this to perfection.

Midway through his presentation, he felt the crowd's energy starting to dip. Sensing this, he created a rule out of thin air:

He told the audience, "I just got word from the venue staff that I only have a few minutes left to close out this presentation. And if I go over, I'll be fined."

He let that idea settle in for a second. He acted as if he were toiling with his content.

Then, with a rebellious smirk, he leaned into the mic and said, "Well, guess what? I don't care.

I'll happily pay the fine because *you* are more important to me than some fine or a time limit.

This information is too valuable for me to rush through, so if it costs me, so be it."

The energy in the room shifted instantly. The audience cheered, clapped, and locked back in, not just because of what he was saying but because of *why* he was saying it. They felt valued and important—as if he was *breaking a rule for them* because they mattered.

Here's the kicker: There was no fine.

He had made up the rule.

But did the audience feel tricked? No. They felt chosen. They felt that they were worth rebelling for. And that's the key. When people see that you're willing to break a rule *on their behalf*, they don't just listen to you—they root for you.

Want to make an audience feel special? Show them that they're worth bending the rules for.

That's why restaurant waiters who slip you an extra scoop of ice cream without charging you get bigger tips. It's why people love it when a boss lets them leave work early *just because*. It's why we feel a rush when a concert performer "defies the venue" and plays an extra encore song for the fans.

These moments aren't just about breaking rules—they're about creating loyalty, connection, and a feeling of exclusivity.

So the next time you're engaging an audience, ask yourself two questions:

1. *What "rule" can I set…just so I can break it for them?*

2. *How can I show them that I value them enough to step outside the official boundaries?*

Master this, and you won't just hold attention—you'll earn devotion.

Seeing Yourself in Subtle Rebellion

The truth is, subtle rebellion is everywhere—and we've all been part of it.

We've been the ones *leaning in*, captivated by the promise of a rule being bent or a truth being revealed.

We've also been the ones *initiating* it—bending and breaking expectations to create excitement, engagement, or a little bit of magic.

That's why this works. Because subtle rebellion isn't just a gimmick—it's something we all *feel*.

It's why we love it when a teacher throws out the lesson plan to have a real conversation.

It's why we remember the time our parents said, "Tonight you can stay up past your bedtime."

It's why we lean in when someone on stage says, "I wasn't supposed to say this, but…"

It makes us feel something. And when you make people *feel* something, you have their attention.

The Two Keys to Subtle Rebellion

1. It Doesn't Push—It Pulls

The most powerful moments of rebellion aren't forced. They *lure* people in. They make them feel like insiders, like coconspirators in something special.

2. It's Not About Destruction—It's About Disruption

Subtle rebellion isn't about breaking rules for the sake of breaking them. It's about disrupting expectations in a way that sparks engagement, curiosity, and connection.

So the next time you're in front of a crowd—whether in a stadium, in a boardroom, or at your dinner table—think about the rules.

Which ones can you bend? Which ones can you tease? Which ones can you create—just so you can break them?

When you master this art, you don't just hold attention. You command it.

You don't just entertain. You captivate.

You don't just deliver a message. You make people *feel* it. And that?

That's how you become a **master of the crowd**.

Rewind and Reflect Section: Mastering Subtle Rebellion

Key Takeaways

- Subtle rebellion—when used with purpose—can instantly capture attention and curiosity.

- Challenging expectations helps you stand out in environments where sameness dominates.

- The most powerful disruptors don't reject rules entirely—they bend them with intention. - Controlled defiance creates impact when it's aligned with your core message and mission. - To become a rebel with a cause, you must understand both the rules and when to break them.

Reflection Questions

- When have you seen someone break expectations in a way that made people lean in?

- What societal or professional rules have you followed by default and why?

- Where in your life or work would disruption help people better receive your message?

- How can you use subtle rebellion to stand out without alienating your audience?

- What message are you truly trying to deliver—and how can rebellion serve it?

Action Steps

- Identify one outdated norm in your industry or community. Challenge it in your next presentation or project.

- Brainstorm three ways you could surprise your audience with a fresh, unexpected approach that aligns with your message.

- Watch or study a disruptor you admire. Note how they use defiance with strategy and intent.

Power Concept

True influence isn't about breaking rules—it's about bending expectations with purpose. Subtle rebellion isn't defiance for attention—it's disruption with direction.

Chapter 5

Mastering Engagement: InterActivation

"The audience isn't waiting to be impressed, they're waiting to be included."

The Death of Passive Participation

How many times have you sat through a presentation, sermon, lecture, or performance and felt completely detached? The speaker might have had great content, but the delivery was flat. The energy was nonexistent, and the connection was nowhere to be found.

We've all been there, trapped in a one-way communication stream where someone is talking *at* us instead of *with* us.

The truth is that passive audiences are disengaged audiences, and disengaged audiences forget everything you said the moment they leave.

On the flip side, have you ever been so engaged at a game or concert that you lost your voice, as if your energy was the determining factor in whether your team won? Have you ever been so in tune with a presenter that you could finish their sentences with excitement? What's the difference?

In one situation, you were talked to. In the other, you were talked with. In one, they performed for you. In the other, you all performed together.

This is a principle I call "**InterActivation**."

For years, I have questioned why some moments capture the energy of a crowd so completely that they become legendary, while others fall flat. I have found that the difference isn't just confidence, talent, or even ability—it's **InterActivation**.

Defining InterActivation

InterActivation is the science and art of transforming passive audiences into active participants through interactive cues, emotional connections, and strategic engagement. It's about moving beyond traditional engagement to create an experience where the audience feels ownership over the energy, direction, and outcome of the event.

When people contribute to an experience, they value it more. This is a concept I learned in real time in LA at one of the biggest sporting events in the country.

InterActivating SoFi Stadium

Let me take you to SoFi Stadium in Inglewood, California. The College Football National Championship: University of Georgia (UGA) versus Texas Christian University (TCU). The stakes were monumental, the energy electric, and I had the honor of being the in-game DJ and host. The goal was clear: Keep over 70,000 fans engaged, energized, and fully immersed in the experience.

Before the game, we gathered for a pregame strategy meeting led by Bob Becker, one of the greatest producers of live events. Bob, who is the Michael Jordan of live events, has orchestrated countless history-making, unforgettable spectacles. As he shared his vision for the game, it wasn't just about the action on the field. It was about engaging the fans and making them feel that they were part of something larger than life.

When Bob asked for ideas to amp up fan interaction, I saw an opportunity to create magic. Drawing on the extensive decoding and research I had done on both schools' fan cultures, I knew that both UGA and TCU prided themselves on a dance called the "Swag Surf." UGA fans claimed they had originated it, while TCU fans argued they had perfected it with the largest Swag Surf in history. It was a perfect rivalry waiting to happen.

I pitched the idea: "Let's have a Swag Surf battle, stadium-wide. We'll challenge the fans to prove who does it best."

Bob raised an eyebrow and asked, "How are you going to get seventy thousand people to join in?"

I grinned and replied, "By challenging them to challenge each other. This isn't just about a dance—it's about their school pride, their identity, and their culture." This was a completely new idea for Bob, and he was taking a chance on me, so I couldn't let him down.

When the moment came, I grabbed the mic and, facing the camera, I said, "All right, family, I hear there's some debate over who does the Swag Surf the best. Is it the originators, UGA?"

Half the stadium erupted in cheers. "Or is it the innovators, TCU?" The other half screamed back.

"Well, let's settle this once and for all. Everyone on your feet! Prove to the world who's got the best Swag Surf!"

I played the song, and the stadium transformed. Entire sections moved in perfect unison, swaying and cheering. Cheerleaders, mascots, and even assistant coaches joined in. It wasn't just a dance—it was a cultural moment, a collective expression of pride and connection.

Bob Becker later told me, "In all my years of doing this, I've never seen anything like that."

This wasn't just about entertainment—it was about **InterActivating the crowd**. The fans weren't passive spectators anymore. They were **contributors** with a responsibility to the atmosphere, their team, and the memory of that night.

The Science of InterActivation

At its core, InterActivation works because it taps into how the human brain is wired.

Neuroscience tells us that our brains aren't wired for passive observation. Instead, they're wired for participation. When we actively engage in something—whether answering a question, chanting with a crowd, or moving with intention—our brains release dopamine, the neurochemical associated with pleasure, motivation, and memory.[9] This isn't just about entertainment. It's about creating emotional hooks that anchor your message in the minds of your audience.

---

[9] John J. Ratey and Eric Hagerman, *Spark: The Revolutionary New Science of Exercise and the Brain* (Little, Brown and Company, 2008); John Medina, *Brain Rules: 12 Principles for Surviving and Thriving at Work, Home, and School* (Pear Press, 2008).

That's why the most unforgettable experiences in our lives are often the ones where we didn't just observe—we played a part. We felt seen. We contributed. We mattered. Whether those moments were shouting the chorus back at the artist at a live concert, solving a problem in front of others in a classroom, or getting pulled into a story at a lecture when the speaker asked a question that hit home, they *stuck*.

In fact, in *Brain Rules*, developmental molecular biologist John Medina shows that the brain is far more likely to retain information when that information is emotionally charged and physically engaging.[10] This is why passive lectures fade fast—but interactive storytelling, handson workshops, or surprise elements in a speech stay with us for years.

Real-World InterActivation Examples

- **Live audience polling:** Whether it's in a keynote or webinar, allowing the audience to instantly weigh in creates a feedback loop that boosts attention and emotional buy-in.

- **Unexpected movement prompts:** A speaker might ask everyone to stand and high-five the person next to them

---

[10] Medina, *Brain Rules*.

or shift to a different side of the room based on a question. This brief movement boosts focus and resets attention.

- **Call-and-response moments:** Think of a DJ hyping up a crowd or a spoken word poet repeating a line until the audience joins in. This shared rhythm builds unity and energy.

- **Choose-your-own-adventure moments:** When a speaker lets the audience choose the next story or theme to explore—based on a show of hands or app voting—it creates ownership and involvement.

InterActivation isn't a gimmick. It's science. It's strategy. And most importantly, it's respect. It says to your audience, "You matter here. You're not just here to consume, you're here to cocreate this moment with me."

The 12th Man

InterActivation thrives in competitive sports environments, with the Seattle Seahawks' 12th man phenomenon serving as a prime example. The Seahawks have cultivated a culture where fans are not mere spectators but an integral part of the team's performance. This is evident at Lumen Field, renowned as one of the NFL's loudest stadiums, where the architecture amplifies crowd noise, creating a formidable atmosphere for visiting teams. From 2002 to 2012, opposing teams committed 143 false-start penalties at Lumen Field, underscoring the tangible impact of fan engagement on game dynamics.[11]

The Seahawks' fans, collectively known as the "12s," have twice set Guinness World

Records for the loudest crowd roar at a sports stadium. On September 15, 2013, they reached 136.6 decibels during a game against the San Francisco 49ers, and on December 2, 2013, they surpassed their own record with 137.6 decibels against the New Orleans Saints.[12]

This phenomenon exemplifies InterActivation by transforming the audience from passive observers into active participants who feel directly responsible for the event's energy and outcome. When individuals believe their involvement influences the experience, they exhibit heightened investment and engagement.

---

[11] John Parolin, "Three-Point Stance: Seattle Seahawks," ESPN, October 10, 2012, https://www.espn.com/blog/boston/new-england-patriots/post/_/id/4731877/three-point-stance-seattle-seahawks.

[12] Ken Belson, "Seahawks Fans Act as Extra Player, Tormenting Opponents and Eardrums," *New York Times*, January 19, 2014, https://www.nytimes.com/2014/01/20/sports/football/when-fans-turn-up-volumeseahawks-play-with-a-man-advantage.html; Associated Press, "Seattle Fans Set Noise Record in Win Over San Francisco 49ers," NFL.com, September 15, 2013, https://www.nfl.com/news/seattle-fans-set-noise-record-in-winover-san-francisco-49ers-0ap1000000245314; Mark Memmott, "Seahawks Fans Cause Earthquake, Set Noise Record," NPR, December 3, 2013, https://www.npr.org/sections/thetwo-way/2013/12/03/248566190/seahawksfans-cause-earthquake-set-noise-record.

Extending InterActivation Beyond Traditional Settings

The principles of InterActivation are not confined to sports. They can be applied in various contexts to enhance engagement:

- **Educational environments:** In classrooms, teachers who encourage student participation through discussions, group work, and interactive activities often see improved learning outcomes. This active involvement fosters a sense of responsibility and investment in the material.

- **Corporate meetings:** Leaders who solicit input during meetings and encourage collaborative problem-solving create a more dynamic and committed workforce. Employees are more likely to feel valued and engaged when they actively contribute to discussions and decisions.

- **Virtual events:** In the digital realm, webinars that incorporate live polls, Q&A sessions, and interactive chats can transform passive viewers into active participants, enhancing the overall experience and retention of information.

When InterActivation strategies are adopted, various settings can transform audiences from passive listeners to active contributors, enriching the overall experience and fostering a deeper connection to the content or event.

But what if the crowd is too young to even understand responsibility yet?

Could this same concept work in the most difficult settings?

The Toughest Crowd

Ask any teacher which age group is the hardest to keep engaged, and you'll likely hear the same answer: **first and second graders**. Their attention spans are famously fleeting, their energy is boundless, and their developing personalities mean you never quite know what you'll get next. Yet, as challenging as that sounds, it's also the perfect environment to demonstrate the power of InterActivation.

I reached out to an elementary school teacher friend of mine and asked if I could put this concept to the ultimate test. The goal was to do the most difficult thing in front of the most challenging type of crowd (cue the *Mission Impossible* theme song). My mission? Teaching a lesson on following directions and listening attentively to a class of spirited six- and seven-yearolds. If you're a parent of one, you absolutely understand how troublesome and problematic this task could be.

As I walked into the class, I was determined to craft my hello in a way that the students couldn't turn away from. Before I even introduced myself, I placed a big grab bag of candy on the desk and announced, "This is a bag of the best candy in the world. You may have a chance to reach in and grab something out—but only if everyone participates."

Then I mentioned, "In life, paying attention and being able to follow directions can bring not just good things to your life but *great* things. Today, it could bring you a piece of some of the *greatest* candy in the world."

Here were the rules:

- Every time I said the word "**great**," the students had to clap once.

- The first student to clap would get to pick a piece of candy from the bag.

- If everyone clapped at the same time, I'd choose someone at random to grab a candy.

- If nobody clapped, they'd all earn extra homework.

We began. I had barely finished saying, "My name is Mr. McCoy, and my *great*-grandfather—" when a boy jumped up and put his hands together in a loud clap. I pointed him to the grab bag, and he proudly fished out a Snickers bar. Instantly, every kid in the room snapped to attention, eager to be the next to score a piece of candy.

By gamifying participation, I got these young students to transition from passive observers to active contributors and aspiring winners. They listened to each word I spoke, anticipating the moment I'd say "great" again. Toward the end of the lesson, I brought out a big, delicious sucker and asked, "How many people remember every word I said?" Of course, all hands went up because the students assumed if they got the answer right, they'd get the sucker.

So, I asked three questions from my presentation. All hands went up for every question. All questions were answered. I awarded the most energetic student the sucker. Just like that, I'd proven the power of **InterActivation** on one of the toughest audiences around.

Mission accomplished.

This simple yet complex exercise is what InterActivation is all about.

You offer a clear incentive for engagement, and suddenly, the audience (or, in this case, the classroom) has buy-in. They adopt a responsibility to listen, respond, and uphold the shared rules that promise a reward. Whether you're teaching first graders, hosting a corporate event, or commanding a stadium, the principle is the same: When people take on an active role, they're no longer just sitting through an experience—they're invested in it. That's when real engagement begins, and that's when even the shortest attention spans light up with a sense of responsibility, excitement, and shared purpose.

Why Passive Audiences Tune Out

Research in cognitive science shows that people retain more information when they actively participate in an experience rather than passively consume it. Studies in educational psychology have found that students who engage in active learning techniques (such as discussion, problemsolving, and hands-on activities) retain nearly twice as much information as those who simply listen to a lecture.[13]

In entertainment, this principle is even more crucial. When audiences are passively watching, their attention drifts. This is why long speeches lose their impact, why concerts with little crowd interaction feel dull, and why sporting events with no crowd engagement lack electricity. The energy isn't just in the performer—it's in the audience. The best entertainers, speakers, and crowd masters know how to tap into that.

---

[13] Scott Freeman et al., "Active Learning Increases Student Performance in Science, Engineering, and

Mathematics," *Proceedings of the National Academy of Sciences of the United States of America* 111, no. 23 (2014), 8410–15, https://doi.org/10.1073/pnas.1319030111; Michelene T. H. Chi, "Active-Constructive-Interactive: A Conceptual Framework for Differentiating Learning Activities," *Topics in Cognitive Science* 1, no. 1 (2009): 73–105, https://doi.org/ 10.1111/j.1756-8765.2008.01005.x.

The IKEA Effect and Mirror Neurons

One of the most compelling psychological principles supporting InterActivation is the **IKEA effect**, the idea that people place a higher value on things they have actively contributed to creating. According to research published in the *Journal of Consumer Psychology*, when individuals participate in a process—whether that involves assembling furniture or engaging in a performance—they develop a stronger sense of ownership and emotional investment.[14]

Another key component of InterActivation lies in mirror neurons, the parts of the brain that mimic the actions of others.[15] When an audience sees an engaged, activated crowd, they naturally want to join in. This is why a stadium wave spreads, why laughter is contagious in a comedy club, and why participation creates a heightened emotional response.

But the key is **deliberate activation**. It's not enough to simply hope your audience participates. You must **engineer** opportunities for them to be part of the moment.

---

[14] Michael I. Norton, Daniel Mochon, and Dan Ariely, "The IKEA Effect: When Labor Leads to Love," *Journal of Consumer Psychology* 22, no. 3 (2012), 453–60, https://doi.org/10.1016/j.jcps.2011.08.002.

[15] Giacomo Rizzolatti and Laila Craighero, "The Mirror-Neuron System," *Annual Review of Neuroscience* 27 (2004): 169–92, https://doi.org/10.1146/annurev.neuro.27.070203.144230.

How to InterActivate Any Audience

Here's how you can turn passive listeners into active participants and create an experience that sticks:

1. Use Call-and-Response Magic

If you've ever been to a Black church, a hip-hop concert, or a political rally, you've witnessed the power of call-and-response. This technique engages audiences in real time, making them cocreators of the experience.

When I DJ, I use this constantly. If I say, "When I say 'turn up,' you say 'right now!'"— the crowd is no longer just watching me. They are a part of the show. Their voices, their energy, and their reactions shape how the moment unfolds.

Key tip: Start simple. Call-and-response doesn't have to be complicated. A classic example is "Somebody scream!" If the audience complies, you know they're with you. If not, you adjust and build toward that moment.

2. Break the Fourth Wall

In theater, the fourth wall is the imaginary barrier between performers and the audience. Great entertainers consistently break this wall. Think about Kevin Hart pointing out an audience member's reaction during a comedy special or Michael Jackson reaching out for a fan's hand during a performance. These moments don't just engage one person—they engage the entire crowd, making them feel included.

Key tip: Make eye contact, point people out, and acknowledge the audience directly. A simple "I see you vibing in the front row!" can ignite a wave of participation.

3. Make Movement Mandatory

One of the best ways to engage an audience is to get them to physically move. Science backs this up—kinesthetic engagement (using movement to learn and interact) boosts memory and emotional connection.[16]

In stadiums, it's the wave. In concerts, it's jumping up and down. In a corporate event, it might involve getting people to stand and raise their hands in response to a question. The key is that motion creates emotion.

4. Trigger Emotional Buy-In

The most powerful audience engagement occurs when people feel emotionally connected. That's why fans at a championship game scream louder than those at a preseason game—there's more at stake.

---

[16] Daniel Casasanto and Katinka Dijkstra, "Motor Action and Emotional Memory," *Cognition* 115, no. 1 (2010): 179–185, https://doi.org/10.1016/j.cognition.2009.11.002.

Speakers, musicians, and performers can achieve the same effect by creating moments of shared emotion. A moment of shared emotion might be a heartfelt personal story, a moment of silence for a cause, or a powerful buildup leading to an epic payoff.

The Audience Is the Star

When you step onto a stage—whether that's in a stadium, a boardroom, a classroom, or even a family gathering—remember this: It's never just about you. It's about your audience. The more you bring your audience into the moment, the more unforgettable the experience will be. The best leaders, performers, and speakers don't just communicate—they cocreate an experience.

True mastery of engagement comes not from commanding attention but from activating the room. You're not just speaking, performing, or presenting—you're unlocking energy, orchestrating emotions, and facilitating a moment that people feel personally connected to.

When you harness InterActivation, the energy in the room isn't something you generate alone—it's something you unleash in others.

The Difference Between Forgettable and Legendary

There's a reason some events feel hollow while others stay with us forever. Some speeches receive polite applause, while others make history. Some concerts are "good," while others become the stuff of legend.

The difference?

Participation. Ownership. Emotional investment.

People don't remember what they watched—they remember what they felt **a part of**. They recall where they were when they screamed the loudest, when they clapped instinctively, and when they felt **so engaged that they lost track of time**.

The experience is no longer **theirs to consume**—it's theirs to **own**.

That's what you're after.

From Passive to Purposeful

When you activate your audience, you give them purpose. You make them responsible for the energy. You turn **listeners into believers, watchers into contributors**, and **spectators into participants**.

And the best part? This applies to **any** audience, anywhere.

- A **CEO giving a keynote** can either deliver a speech or create a moment that makes the audience feel **invested** in the company's future.

- A **teacher in a classroom** can either lecture or **bring students into the lesson** so they feel like part of the learning process.

- A **coach** can either yell plays from the sidelines or **activate the team's sense of responsibility** so they fight for every inch.

- A **pastor in a church** can either preach a sermon or **ignite a response** that makes people feel personally involved in the message.

- **The setting doesn't matter. The principle does.**

The Power of an Activated Audience

An audience that is truly **activated** is one that won't just cheer in the moment—they will carry that energy with them **long after the moment is over**. Think about that:

- A concert where the crowd sings every word long after the music stops.

- A speech where people leave not just inspired but ready to take action.

- A championship game where the fans feel that they played a role in the outcome.

- A moment where the energy in the room is so electric, it becomes a story people tell for years.

That's what makes the difference. That's what turns a simple event into an unforgettable movement.

Your Challenge: InterActivate Your Next Moment

The next time you step in front of a group—any group—ask yourself three simple but profound questions:

1. **Am I speaking at them, or am I speaking with them?**

2. **Am I controlling the energy, or am I unlocking theirs?**

3. **Are they just watching, or are they part of the moment?**

If you can master these three things, you'll never just hold attention again—you'll create moments that resonate long after they're over. That's what InterActivation is. And that's how you master the crowd.

Rewind and Reflect Section: Mastering Engagement Through InterActivation

Key Takeaways

- Engagement is not just about entertainment—it's about interaction and emotional connection.

- Audiences become energized when they feel seen, involved, and vital to the experience.

- Transforming passive listeners into active participants creates unforgettable moments. - The energy of the crowd can be led, shaped, and intensified with strategic cues.

- InterActivation is the difference between performing *for* a crowd and connecting *with* them.

Reflection Questions

- When have you been part of a crowd that felt alive, and what triggered that connection?

- What methods have you used to involve your audience, and how effective were they?

- How can you create more shared experiences that bring people into the moment with you?

- What barriers might prevent your audience from participating, and how can you lower them?

- How would your next talk or event change if your goal was activation, not just applause?

Action Steps

- Design one interactive moment in your next talk, event, or meeting where the audience becomes a part of the experience. - Test a simple engagement technique (like call-and-response or live polling) in a small setting and note the energy shift.

- Analyze a recording of yourself presenting. Note every moment the audience is passive, and brainstorm how to activate them.

Power Concept

The most memorable moments don't happen to your audience—they happen with them.

Engagement isn't about performance—it's about interactive participation.

Chapter 6

Mastering Music's Influence: Language Beyond Lyrics

"Music is the universal language of mankind."
—Henry Wadsworth Longfellow

The Soundtrack of Influence

It was Friday night—dad and daughters night. I'd promised my daughters, who were then six and 10, that I'd take them to the movies. They'd picked out *The Secret Life of Pets*, an animated film featuring Kevin Hart and other stars. The movie itself was lighthearted and funny, full of hilarious moments that had my daughters laughing throughout the entire film. It was a great time, and I was happy to have shared it with them.

As the movie neared its end, the closing scene arrived. All the pets, after a chaotic yet heartwarming adventure, made their way back into their homes just in time for their owners to return and shower them with love. It was one of those classic happily-ever-after moments. But what took me by surprise was the song that began to play during the scene. Bill Withers's "Lovely Day" began to fill the theater, and suddenly, I was overwhelmed with emotion.

Now, to give you some context, every Saturday morning when I was growing up, my mother would wake the entire house up with Bill Withers's "Lovely Day" blaring from the stereo as loud as it could go. At the time, I hated the smell of Clorox bleach and Windex filling the house while I was forced to clean, but that song was a part of it—part of that ritual that tied us together as a family.

After my mother passed away, I started playing that song every Saturday morning. And as I did, I found myself transported back in time to those mornings when everything felt simple, and I was with her. The memories flooded back—the love, the connection, the togetherness. It was a time I cherished and missed dearly.

So, there I was, sitting in the movie theater, watching a children's animated film, when the same song played. I was in tears. My daughters, completely unaware of the deeper connection I had to that song, asked, "What's wrong, Dad? Did you not like the movie?"

"I loved the movie," I said. "But the choice to play that song? I loved it even more. It brought me back to a place I didn't know I missed so much."

Has this ever happened to you? Have you ever been transported from where you were, physically and emotionally, to another place entirely through the power of music?

Music's ability to evoke memories and emotions is a phenomenon that transcends mere sound. In that moment, as "Lovely Day" played and my heart swelled with love and longing, I realized how deeply music can anchor us to the past and connect us to what we've lost or longed for. Music doesn't just accompany moments—it creates them. It moves us. And as I sat in that theater, surrounded by my daughters, I experienced firsthand the undeniable power of music to reach deep into our souls and awaken memories we didn't know we had.

The Neuroscience of Memory and Music

Consider the following when it comes to the relationship between music and the brain:

- **The role of the hippocampus:** The hippocampus, the brain's memory center, is heavily involved in processing music. It links melodies to past experiences, explaining why we often associate songs with specific life events.[17]

---

[17] Jörn-Henrik Jacobsen et al., "Why Musical Memory Can Be Preserved in Advanced Alzheimer's Disease," *Brain: A Journal of Neurology* 138, no. 8 (2015): 2438–50, https://doi.org/10.1093/brain/awv135.

- **Dopamine and the pleasure response:** Music triggers the release of dopamine, the "feel-good" neurotransmitter. This explains why hearing a favorite song can elevate mood and create a sense of joy or nostalgia.

- **Music as a mnemonic device:** Studies show that music enhances learning and recall. This is why jingles are effective in advertising and why students use songs to memorize facts.

Language Beyond Lyrics

Henry Wadsworth Longfellow, a 19th-century poet and literary figure, once said, "Music is the universal language of mankind."[18] I believe that sentiment still rings true today. Whether you're pounding the bongos in Brazil or attempting karaoke in Korea, music speaks louder than my uncle at Thanksgiving dinner—and that's saying something.

Harnessing the universal language of music allows us to engage audiences on levels that words alone cannot achieve. Similar to the whistle from my childhood story in chapter 1, which captivated the entire playground regardless of language, a simple sound can transcend words. Whether you're on the basketball

---

[18] Henry Wadsworth Longfellow, *Outre-Mer: A Pilgrimage Beyond the Sea* (William D. Ticknor & Co., 1846), 202.

court in China or the soccer field in Venezuela, the whistle signifies the same pause and attention. Everyone understands its signal, demonstrating how certain sounds become universally recognized cues.

I've found compelling evidence of this power in my personal experiences. I've traveled to countries where the locals didn't speak the same language as I did, yet we could all keep in rhythm to a shared beat. I've been in places where my words were unfamiliar, yet our voices could unite in melody and harmonize together. Music serves as a common thread linking races, ages, genders, and backgrounds. Given this universal appeal, why not harness music to our advantage? Music stands as a unifying force, possessing the power to engage, evoke emotion, and foster connections on levels that words alone cannot achieve.

Music is humanity's language used to communicate where words run out.

I've seen this language spoken in many forms. I've toured with numerous artists and hosted and DJed at thousands of stadiums, arenas, concert venues, and clubs around the world. I've performed across a wide array of genres—from hip-hop to country, pop to gospel, R&B to EDM, reggae to salsa. I've been blessed with the opportunity to use this language in almost every genre.

Artists and brands ask me all the time, **"How do you thrive in front of such diverse audiences and different genres?"**

Musically, here's my secret: I've found that people fall in love with their favorite artists between the ages of 17 and 21. If you think of your favorite artist or song right now, there's a good chance it stems from that age range. When I step in front of an audience, whether in a DJ booth or as a host, I estimate when the majority of the crowd, or a specific portion of the crowd, was between the ages of 17 and 21. Once I figure that out, I have a base to work from, and I gauge live reactions and responses to the songs played, letting the crowd's energy determine where we go from there.

When I walk into a room, it's as if I read the room's temperature. I can sense the mood based on how people react to certain music. As I play different tracks, I observe how the audience responds, whether it's through clapping, dancing, or sheer energy. Music acts as my personal guide. It helps me understand the vibe, and from there, I can lead the crowd to where they need to go emotionally, whether that's hyping them up, calming them down, or stirring them into action. This is how I maintain control over an experience—through the magic of music.

The World's Greatest Entertainer, Doug E. Fresh

I learned this firsthand from one of my heroes, Doug E. Fresh. He's not just a pioneer in hip-hop. He's a living masterclass in the power of performance. I've had the honor of rocking countless shows with him, and over time, he's poured into me lessons that go far beyond music—they're about impact. One of the most powerful truths he ever shared with me is that music isn't just what you play—it's what you *show*. The most unforgettable performances are felt, not heard.

They communicate without saying a word.

Doug once broke down the role choreography played in the early days of hip-hop. For example, with Big Daddy Kane, it wasn't just about syncing dance moves—it was about sending a message. When Kane, Scoob, and Scrap would hit the stage and execute clean, rehearsed movements, that told the audience *"We prepared for this moment."* That unity was its own form of language, a statement of purpose and professionalism that transcended the lyrics.

Doug E. Fresh also schooled me on the brilliance of Rock 'n' Roll Hall of Famers Public Enemy. Their influence didn't stop at the music. It extended to how they *presented* themselves. When that group took the stage with military precision, flanked by the S1Ws, it wasn't just powerful—it was commanding. That visual impact alone told the crowd they were witnessing something serious, something organized, something worthy of attention. As Doug put it, when you move with unity, people assume you lead with clarity. And that *leadership* is what the audience buys into, often before a single bar is dropped.

Those experiences taught me something vital: that some of the most powerful forms of communication don't involve language at all. A gesture, a formation, a beat drop at the perfect moment—these can say more than a whole verse ever could. That's the essence of the language beyond lyrics. It's a way of connecting with people on a level deeper than words. And once I understood that, it opened the door to one of the most powerful tools I use today to activate any audience.

The Live-Survey Method

I remember it as if it were yesterday—we were doing an NAACP event in Detroit and had just gotten off a plane and walked into the venue. Doug and I hadn't had an opportunity to read the crowd, so I was a little apprehensive. As we walked up, I plugged in and introduced him, and he did the most incredibly savvy and strategic thing I had ever seen.

He started by engaging the crowd by calling out age groups: "Twenty and over, make some noise! Thirty and over, make some noise," and so on. Then he asked which era had the best music. After that, he asked me to play songs from each era he had just called out. By conducting the survey live, he could determine which age group screamed the loudest. Once he identified the majority, he knew exactly where to start and end the party—genius! Just as Doug E. Fresh adapted his music strategy in real time, businesses can do the same by integrating music into their customer experience.

This live-survey method is an incredibly smart tool for reading your audience and determining their musical preferences in real time. It's a simple yet effective way to get instant feedback and then use that data to tailor the experience. Imagine walking into a venue, starting a conversation with your audience through music, and immediately being able to read their response. By using this method, Doug E. Fresh was able to bring the energy that the crowd needed at the exact right moment, making the experience more engaging and memorable.

Corporate Adaptation

Imagine translating this concept to a corporate setting. Can you envision walking into Target, greeted by large buttons on the walls labeled with each decade from the '60s through the modern day? As people walk in, they just tap the button of the era with which they identify. You would have constant awareness of the era of music that your shoppers love.

Let's say, at 1 p.m. on a Saturday afternoon, you check the analytics and find that 75% of your shoppers represent the '80s era of music. You could immediately play an '80s-curated playlist, enhancing the shopping experience for 75% of your customers.

Research suggests that this familiarity and preference can encourage consumers to spend more time shopping.[19]

Can you imagine how profitable that information could be?

This is exactly what Doug E. Fresh did live on stage. He used a live survey to determine which music the audience resonated with most and then live scored the rest of the event with it.

Brilliant!

The key to Doug's success was in understanding his audience, not just reading the crowd's energy from their actions but

---

[19] Richard Yalch and Eric R. Spangenberg, "Effects of Store Music on Shopping Behavior," *Journal of Consumer Marketing* 7, no. 2 (1990): 55–63, https://doi.org/10.1108/EUM0000000002577; Francine V. Garlin and Katherine Owen, "Setting the Tone with the Tune: A Meta-Analytic Review of the Effects of Background Music in Retail Settings," *Journal of Business Research* 59, no. 6 (2006): 755–64, https://doi.org/10.1016/j.jbusres.2006.01.013.

also understanding their emotional response to the music. Once you know what connects with your audience, you can push them further into the experience. And this is where the magic happens. Whether it's in the middle of a concert, a live event, or a customer experience, the right music can elevate your message and amplify your impact.

The Science Behind Music and Memory

Music's ability to evoke emotion is not just anecdotal. It's a scientific phenomenon. Professor Petr Janata from the University of California, Davis, discovered that familiar music activates regions in the brain associated with autobiographical memories, evoking profound emotions and vivid recollections.[20] This is why a song from our teenage years can transport us back in time, complete with the emotions and sensations of that period. Memory and emotion are intricately linked through music. Applying this to audience engagement means that it can be helpful to choose songs that resonate with your audience's significant eras, thereby deepening their connection to your message. Familiarity fosters comfort, and comfort fosters engagement. This information serves as a powerful reminder that music doesn't just accompany our lives—it underscores them.

---

[20] Petr Janata, "The Neural Architecture of Music-Evoked Autobiographical Memories," *Cerebral Cortex* 19, no. 11 (2009): 2579–94, https://doi.org/10.1093/cercor/bhp008.

This is precisely why music is so effective when it comes to creating memorable experiences. When you understand the psychological and emotional triggers music can ignite, you can use it as a tool to make your message stick. Whether it's creating a nostalgic connection or triggering a specific emotional state, music has the ability to solidify a moment in time and make it unforgettable.

Movie Music Magic

Imagine a horror movie without its chilling score. The scene would shift from terrifying to typical, reducing moments that might have been tense to simple views of farms or country roads. It's the well-composed score that transforms these images, infusing them with tension, fear, or anticipation, and elevating them beyond their visual simplicity. Composers like John Carpenter showcase this brilliantly. With *Halloween*, Carpenter's haunting minimalism evokes unease and suspense, turning ordinary suburban streets into settings of dread.

However, it is Hans Zimmer, my personal favorite, whose work consistently demonstrates the emotive power of music. Zimmer's ability to provoke soaring triumph or deep contemplation through his scores enhances films like *The Lion King* and *Inception*, allowing the audience to fully feel the emotional weight of the narrative through music.

The Batman trilogy stands out the most to me. In *The Dark Knight*, a film directed by Christopher Nolan, Zimmer, along with James Newton Howard, was able to musically make you hate the Joker and love him at the same time! The fact that Zimmer and Howard composed music that could simultaneously convey humor, evil, self-righteousness, and misguided passion, all while having a threatening quality, is unbelievable. It was almost as if their original score guided listeners emotionally on how to feel about what they were seeing.

So here's the question: If music is so powerful in guiding and magnifying the emotional experience on screen, why wouldn't we harness its potential in the world of brands, personal storytelling, and especially presentations? Just as a film score boosts a movie's narrative and deepens the viewer's emotional connection, music can enhance your message, boost your own narrative, and make your message more influential and memorable. If music can extend shopping sprees or dinners, it can undoubtedly convey your message or sell your product.

Strategic Use of Music in Brand Recall

Years ago, brands began harnessing this power by creating catchy jingles for commercials. These memorable melodies, with their addictive rhythms and lyrics, have remained stuck in our brains for years. These tunes are so catchy that sometimes, hearing a commercial once is all it takes to memorize its jingle.

Take McDonald's, for example. Brand recall is a powerful result of well-designed jingles, and McDonald's mastery of this is evident with their famous jingle, "Ba-da-ba-ba-ba." No matter where you are, hearing those notes immediately conjures thoughts of McDonald's and the joy

and nostalgia associated with it. This instant recognition ties the brand to happy emotions, creating a deep and lasting consumer bond.

Now, imagine if you could harness this power for your own product or content. Envision a rhythm, a sound, or a musical cue that embodies your brand. By educating your audience about this musical representation of your brand, you create a powerful link. The more this connection is reinforced, the more inseparable your sound and brand become. Whether on a plane, at a convention, in a church, or on the subway, the moment someone hears that sound, your brand comes to mind.

This strategic use of music can create a deep connection between your brand and consumers. This is the secret sauce to ensuring that your brand remains present in the lives and minds of your audience long after your interaction.

The Giggle King

Personally, I have been blessed with a particularly unique laugh. My brothers would call me the giggle king because my laugh is a high-pitched giggle. As I progressed in my career with big brands like the LA Rams, the USC Trojans, the LA Sparks, Coca-Cola, and BET, and when I was on air Monday through Friday on 102.3 KJLH FM, my uncontrollable high-pitched giggle became an unintentional trademark.

After a few events, people would walk up to me everywhere, trying to mimic my laugh. Initially, I was offended, until one of my mentors, Buster Brown, told me to own it. He said, "No matter where people are, if they hear your giggle on that mic, they will know they're in good hands and in for a great time."

Practical Applications and Techniques

Here are some proven strategies—each backed by real-world moments and audience-tested applications—to effectively incorporate music into your presentations, performances, and communications.

Choosing the Right Tracks

Use familiar or era-specific music to evoke emotional connection. Align your musical selection with the theme of your message to deepen resonance.

Real-World Example At a corporate anniversary event, there were some unspoken questions floating in the room about the company's longevity and direction. To shift the atmosphere, I cued up "Don't Stop Believing'" by Journey as guests entered the room. Instantly, heads nodded, smiles spread, and the energy shifted. The nostalgia was real—but so was the message: *Keep believing in this brand, this team, this mission.* The track became a silent rallying cry and grounded the event with a powerful emotional anchor.

Applying Contextual Mood Setting

Adjust tempo and genre to match the emotional tone of the environment. Slow, instrumental music supports reflection, while high-energy tracks inspire motivation and movement.

Real-World Example

At a nonprofit fundraiser, just before we asked the room for donations, I played a soft instrumental piano piece in the background. It set a serious, delicate tone and helped prepare the audience emotionally for the ask. You could feel the room soften—attention focused, hearts opened. That small sound choice paved the way for generosity, connection, and a more meaningful moment.

Using Interactive Sound Cues

Use music as a tool for audience activation. Brief audio clips or hooks can prompt crowd responses, creating real-time connection.

Real-World Example

At a high school pep rally, I turned *"DAY-O!"* from "The Banana Boat Song" into a live chant trigger. Every time I dropped the iconic "Dayyyyy-o!" into the mix, the students had to shout it back—*louder than before*. By the third round, the entire gym was echoing like a stadium. The chant was simple, fun, and deeply engaging. And best of all—it was theirs.

Layering Music in Digital Presentations

Enhance virtual sessions with subtle background tracks to prevent drop-offs in attention and bring flow between topics.

Real-World Example

During a virtual sales meeting, I layered a mellow lo-fi beat beneath the welcome slides to give the session an immediate vibe. Then I used crisp transition sound cues between segments to hold attention and reset focus. What could've been just another muted Zoom call became a session that felt intentional, upbeat, and alive.

Implementing Feedback and Adaptation

Let audience energy guide your music use. Be flexible and observant—adjust in real time to strengthen connection and maximize emotional response.

Real-World Example

In a group fitness class I DJed, the crowd started to lag when a slower track came on. I watched body language dip, and without missing a beat, I pivoted into a high-tempo EDM set. The room flipped in seconds—momentum restored, energy renewed, and smiles back in motion. Music isn't just atmosphere. It's a tool of leadership when used in real time.

The Harmonious Edge

Music possesses a unique power—its ability to transcend language and culture, its capacity to evoke deep emotions, and its knack for influencing human behavior. Whether through a memorable jingle defining your brand's identity or a carefully curated playlist engaging your audience, music provides an unmatched pathway to connect, captivate, and mobilize.

By exploring age-related music preferences, emotional melodies, and rhythmic messaging, we've uncovered how these elements can elevate ordinary interactions into extraordinary experiences. Just as Longfellow saw music as a bridge to cultural understanding, we, too, can use it to forge profound connections with our audiences. Harnessing music's universal appeal and its ability to evoke powerful memories means you're not just amplifying your message—you're creating soundtracks that leave lasting impressions. The next time you step onto a stage, enter a boardroom, or launch a marketing campaign, ask yourself:

Am I just playing music, or am I using it to shape an unforgettable experience?

Because those who master music's influence don't just entertain—they transform moments into memories, and they **master the crowd.**

Rewind and Reflect Section: Mastering Music's Influence

Key Takeaways

- Music is a universal language that communicates emotion beyond words.

- The right sound can shift a room's energy instantly—activating memory, mood, and movement.

- Strategically used, music strengthens emotional connection with any crowd.

- Beyond lyrics, the music's rhythm, tempo, and tone create subconscious responses in your audience.

- You don't need to be a musician to use music as a tool for deeper impact.

Reflection Questions

- What role has music played in shaping some of your most memorable moments?

- Have you ever used music to influence a mood—yours or someone else's? - What songs or sounds align with the message or feeling you want to deliver to your audience?

- How could you integrate musical energy into your presentations, teaching, or leadership? - What nonverbal tools—like tempo and tone—do you already use that mimic musical influence?

Action Steps

- Curate a playlist that aligns with the tone and energy of your next event, session, or moment of leadership.

  - Experiment with background music or walk-on songs to elevate the vibe and deepen audience engagement.

- Identify three songs that emotionally connect with your message—and use one to set the tone in your next gathering.

Power Concept

"Music doesn't just support the message—it becomes the message."

Chapter 7

Mastering the Surprise: Planned Spontaneity

"Magic lives in the unexpected, and power belongs to the one who controls the shift."

The Power of Surprise

If you're like me, you crave excitement—those jolts of newness that break the rhythm of your everyday life and snap you to attention. It's the same reason we enjoy plot twists in our favorite movies or the moment someone unexpectedly calls our name with good news. Surprise is, at its core, a dynamic force that can transform even the most routine activity into an unforgettable experience.

Great performers, speakers, and leaders know this secret well. They understand that when you embed the unexpected into a presentation, lesson, or performance, you captivate your audience in a way that conventional methods rarely achieve. But how does one master the elusive element of surprise without losing control or coherence?

The answer lies in *planned spontaneity*. Sounds like a contradiction, right? How can something be both planned and spontaneous? Yet it's a deliberate strategy used to inject life into performances, presentations, and shows.

Planned spontaneity is a moment in your presentation that is presented to the audience as a spontaneous or on-the-spot, organic moment but is actually prepared and rehearsed. Its purpose is to ensure a feeling of unpredictability for your crowd while maintaining the structure needed to stay on message. Audiences eat this up because it feels like a freeze-frame moment in time that will never happen again.

Why Our Brains Love Surprise

Before diving into my personal discovery of this powerful technique, let's briefly explore why surprise is so effective. A range of neurological research suggests that our brains are wired to perk up when confronted with a break in the norm.[21] When something *unexpected* happens, our neural pathways fire up with excitement, releasing dopamine—the neurotransmitter associated

---

[21] Wolfram Schultz, "Dopamine Reward Prediction-Error Signalling: A Two-Component Response," *Nature Reviews Neuroscience* 17, no. 3 (2016): 183–95, https://doi.org/10.1038/nrn.2015.26.

with pleasure and reward. This wave of dopamine makes us more receptive, more alert, and more willing to engage with whatever follows. Think of it as your brain's built-in wake-up call. Once you're hooked, you'll hang on to every subsequent moment to see what might happen next.

Planned spontaneity leverages this brain chemistry by intentionally weaving in what seems to be unexpected. When done artfully, it leaves your audience in a state of delightful surprise, suspense, and, most of all, curiosity about what could possibly happen next.

The Eric Roberson Experience: A Lesson in Engagement

Let's transition from the theoretical to the practical with the story of how I encountered this concept firsthand, courtesy of the brilliant singer, songwriter, and performer Eric Roberson.

A Case of Initial Skepticism

Back in 2005, I served as music director for the R&B legend Kenny Lattimore. We were wrapping up a major tour on the East Coast when Kenny suggested something that caught me off guard: "We have some free time tonight. Let's catch Eric Roberson's show. He's one of the greatest performers I've seen in a while, and I want us to take some notes."

I was intrigued but, to be honest, also a bit skeptical. As far as I knew, Eric wasn't a household name with a long track record of mainstream hits. We had just come from performing at large, packed venues—so how could *this* show, on a college campus in DC, possibly teach us anything new? At the time, I was thinking, "We're leaving a big-time stage to see what might be a lesser-known act? Really?"

Yet I trusted Kenny's musical instincts. He's worked with some truly high-caliber artists, and he has a knack for spotting greatness in unexpected places. Little did I know that school would be in session. I had no idea that I was about to see something that would forever change the way I viewed live performances—and audience engagement.

A Venue That Felt Like a Classroom

The location itself was more intimate than I had anticipated. It felt like a club that could double as a student lounge. As soon as I walked in, I noticed the electricity in the room: *Everyone* seemed excited, from the folks who were seeing Eric for the hundredth time to the wide-eyed newcomers like me.

Just before the show started, I overheard two women exchanging excited whispers. They mentioned they'd seen Eric perform just last week—yet here they were again, talking about how they *couldn't wait* to see what he'd do *this* time. If that isn't a testament to a performer's draw, I don't know what is. The internal question that popped into my head was "What's he doing differently from week to week that keeps people coming back?"

Winning Over Skeptics with Inclusion

The lights dimmed. The band started with a soulful groove, each instrument carefully layered into a warm introduction. Then Eric strolled on stage. He could have launched straight into a standard setlist, but instead, he asked the crowd, "Is there anyone *not* from DC?"

You could feel everyone physically lean in, anticipating what was coming next. I was hesitant at first, but being from California, I raised my hand. Others chimed in: "Detroit,"

"Atlanta," "Chicago."

Eric's response was immediate, in rhythm and in key: *"Welcome to the show, welcome to the show, whether from ATL or Chicago,*

Welcome to the show, tonight we're gonna toast

from Detroit to the West Coast."

He spun around toward the band, signaling a rhythmic shift with a quick wave of his hand. In that moment, they seamlessly altered the groove to match his improvised lyrics. Each city, each location, got its own little improvised shout-out. He didn't just mention those places— he *celebrated* them. As a result, the entire crowd felt included, and even those who were new to him (like me) couldn't help but smile ear to ear.

He continued:

"Detroit can get cold, Chi Town's wind will run up on ya,

But we all know it never rains in Southern California."

Now, look—I've put on and attended a ton of concerts, but I'd never seen a performer use the audience's backgrounds in that way so quickly and seamlessly to create an instant connection. Usually, you'll see an artist mention, "Hey, how you feeling, [insert name of city]." But Eric took it a step further. He referenced individuals in the crowd, one by one, weaving them into the show's opening.

Right away, you could see the transformation in the room from casual watchers to engaged participants. Suddenly, we weren't just there to listen to his music. We were part of the story unfolding onstage.

From Doubt to Devotion

I found myself laughing, clapping, and feeling that rush of excitement that only comes from witnessing something truly special. Remember, I had arrived with a healthy dose of skepticism, but in less than five minutes, that melted away into pure admiration. I was hooked.

Eric then moved on to perform a few of his own tracks for the die-hard fans, who sang along to every word. I was content just bobbing my head, appreciating his soulful sound. But then came the *moment*—one that still stands out to me today.

He finished his third song, paused, and turned to address the crowd again, saying, "Let's do something different. Right now, we're going to perform the greatest song in the history of music."

Someone shouted out, "What song is it?"

Without missing a beat, Eric answered, "I don't know yet, because we haven't made it up!"

The Big Surprise Moment: Freestyling with the Crowd

Wait, huh? I remember feeling a mix of confusion and exhilaration. Eric then asked the crowd for topics to write this new song about. People started shouting random words at Eric:

"Love!" a woman yelled.

Eric dismissed it, saying it was too easy.

"Shoelaces!" the same lady yelled.

"Doughnuts!" someone else chimed in. "Gangsters!" I couldn't help myself.

"Hair weaves!" hollered another voice.

This was quite the buffet of unrelated suggestions, yet Eric took it in stride. He gave the band a quick nod and a couple of verbal directions, settling into a new, slow-burning R&B groove. Then he started improvising, weaving each crowd-supplied word into brand-new lyrics on the spot:

"*Sometimes life has you all tied up, twisted in knots in places, Don't let them pull your strings. You're more than shoelaces.*" He turned his attention to the next person:

"*Sweet and petite, but people see through your center, Pass on Dunkin' Donuts, Krispy Kreme is a winner.*" When he finally looked in my direction:

"*Gangsters don't dance, but you know they sang, The low riders know, ain't nuthin' but a G thang.*" And to the woman behind me:

"*She threw love up, and I caught it,*

Leave her hair weave alone. It's hers—she bought it."

The place exploded with applause, laughter, and cheers. In those spontaneous verses, Eric had us hanging on to every word. I was *thrilled* to witness such creative spontaneity right before my eyes. And that's the magic of it—Eric had clearly planned to be spontaneous.

I left the show enlightened, with a notebook scribbled full of observations, determined to apply these principles wherever I could—on stage or off. That night, Eric set a gold standard for crowd engagement, demonstrating how carefully orchestrated moments of planned spontaneity can break down skepticism, transform watchers into participants, and keep everyone craving more.

Pulling Back the Curtain: Planning to Be Spontaneous

Eric captivated the crowd in a way that felt entirely off the cuff. Yet behind that seemingly impromptu performance was a carefully laid plan for spontaneity. Yes, Eric had every intention of creating *moments that felt unrehearsed*, but the structure supporting those moments had been painstakingly prepared in advance. This is planned spontaneity at its finest: deliberately orchestrating an "unpredictable" flourish that locks in your audience's attention, leaves them craving more, and best of all, preserves the integrity of your core message.

The Anatomy of Planned Spontaneity Intention Meets Preparation

Planned spontaneity starts long before you step on stage or walk into a room. You decide, "I'm going to have a moment in my presentation or performance where the crowd thinks I'm doing something entirely off the cuff." Then you practice and refine that moment so it appears seamless. Musicians do this by rehearsing pivot points in the set, teachers do it by thinking through "surprise" activities, and speakers do it by marking transitional spots in their talks where they can detour for anecdotes or mini exercises.

Calculated Freedom

To outsiders, Eric's freestyle session looked like pure creative genius—lyrics plucked from thin air and combined like magic. In reality, he likely had mental frameworks or techniques to recall rhymes, pivot rhythms, and segue from one idea to the next. This is *calculated freedom*: You give yourself room to maneuver in real time, but you have safety nets in place (such as key signatures, familiar chord progressions, and tested transitions) so you don't fall flat.

Inclusion of the Audience

A hallmark of planned spontaneity is purposeful crowd participation. By directly calling on the audience—asking them for song topics, suggestions, or quick feedback—you instantly break the fourth wall. The audience members shift from spectators to *cocreators*, feeling as if they're helping shape something brand new and ephemeral. For Eric, singing about shoelaces and doughnuts wasn't random—it was the perfect hook to pull people in, showcase his skill, and make them feel uniquely seen.

Timing and Pacing

Spontaneity is most effective when it happens at just the right moment—when your audience is ready for a jolt of energy or a shift in focus. Eric didn't jump into the freestyle immediately. He warmed us up with a couple of songs, built trust, and then made his move. You want to sense when the room's collective excitement needs to be elevated, then unleash that well-timed surprise.

Why Planned Spontaneity Works: The Science and Strategy Neurological Hooks

Recall how dopamine rushes through our system whenever we encounter the unexpected. When you weave a spontaneous moment into a structured plan, you *control* that dopamine spike. You essentially program your audience's "wow" response. Their brains light up with curiosity, they become more open and receptive, and they lean forward in their seats, hoping for more.

Emotional Resonance and Memorability

Surprise fosters strong emotional reactions, and those emotions become anchors for memory. Think about your favorite childhood moments. How many involve an element of *surprise* or *unexpected excitement*? Planned spontaneity works exactly the same way. The memory of "I can't believe he made up a song about doughnuts and hair weaves on the spot!" remains etched in your mind for years. Whenever you share that story, you relive the delight. Whenever your audience remembers their own freeze-frame moment, they relive *their* delight—and, importantly, *your message*.

Seamless Integration of the "Wow Factor"

Let's face it: A performance or presentation that's entirely predictable loses momentum quickly. Yet it can be risky to wing it wholly or veer off script to chase spontaneity. With planned spontaneity, you engineer these big "wow" experiences without derailing your larger narrative. It's the best of both worlds—a performance that remains polished and purposeful but still has enough sparkle to generate authentic excitement.

Practical Tips for Injecting Planned Spontaneity

Step 1. Identify Your Moments

First, pinpoint where spontaneity will provide the biggest impact. Is it at the beginning, to establish a high energy level? Midway, to revive an audience's lagging attention? Right before your finale, to leave them buzzing on the way out? *Map it out.* Even a single "spontaneous" moment can make your entire performance memorable.

Step 2. Prepare Your Building Blocks

If you're a musician, preparing might mean practicing certain chord progressions you can slip into naturally. If you're a speaker, rehearse how to pivot into a moment of audience interaction. If you're a teacher, plan a quick, playful quiz or Q&A session. In all cases, keep essential prompts or questions ready so you don't freeze up when spontaneity calls.

Step 3. Invite Audience Participation

As Eric demonstrated, handing the spotlight to your crowd can elevate the energy in the room. Ask for topic suggestions, open the floor to the audience, or hold a quick poll. This tactic requires forethought. What if you get bizarre or off-topic suggestions? How will you gracefully steer them back to your main theme? That's part of your preplanning—building mental "escape routes" or comedic lines so you can handle the unexpected with confidence.

Step 4. Use Anchor Points

Even though it's labeled "spontaneity," you still need anchor points to ensure you return to your core message. Think of these anchors as signposts that keep you from wandering too far off course. Once you've completed your surprise bit, you can smoothly guide the audience back to your main storyline, ensuring cohesion.

Step 5. Practice, but Don't Overpolish

Yes, paradoxical as it sounds, you *can* overpractice spontaneity. The magic lies in leaving just enough unpredictability to feel fresh. Spend time refining your transitions, but allow space for genuine reactions to the crowd or environment. Remember, the authenticity of your surprise is what makes people gasp, laugh, or cheer.

Turning Skeptics into Believers

It's worth emphasizing how powerful planned spontaneity can be for winning over those who initially doubt you or your message. As we saw with Eric's crowd, including newcomers like me has the following benefits:

Establishes trust quickly: When you demonstrate that you're willing to adapt on the spot— whether through improv, acknowledging the crowd, or fielding random suggestions—you position yourself as confident and skilled. Skepticism softens into curiosity.

Includes everyone: By referencing different cities, personal hobbies, or audience shout-outs, you make each individual feel like part of the show. In that instant, it's no longer *your* performance but *our* shared experience.

Sparks word-of-mouth buzz: Once people witness something that appears spontaneously extraordinary, they talk about it. They become your ambassadors, telling others, "You have to see this—it's like nothing you've ever experienced!" That excitement can be contagious, attracting an ever-growing audience.

Surprise as Your Secret Weapon

Planned spontaneity is more than a performance trick. It's a mindset that respects your audience's intelligence and emotional engagement. It says, "I care enough to craft an experience you haven't seen before, one that feels alive and unrepeatable." And when done well, it generates not just entertainment but also a bond—a dynamic sense of community shared among everyone present.

The best part? Anyone can harness this. Whether you're rocking a stadium stage, commanding a corporate boardroom, or running a small classroom, you can sprinkle in an element of the unexpected. Plan it carefully, but deliver it as if it just popped into your head. Watch how quickly the room's energy changes. See how that wave of excitement carries your main message—be it a song, a lesson, or a presentation—far deeper into your audience's hearts and minds than straightforward delivery ever could.

Remember, keep your core structure intact, inject a genuine spirit of creativity, and invite your audience along for the ride. They'll walk away with a lasting memory of that *one magical moment* you gave them. And that's exactly what you want—

something they'll talk about, share with others, and think back on with a smile. That, my friend, is the enduring power of *planned spontaneity.*

As you step into your next performance, lesson, or meeting, remember that the secret to true engagement lies in blending the art of the unexpected with the rigor of careful preparation.

Embrace planned spontaneity as your secret weapon—crafting moments that dazzle with the appearance of on-the-spot genius while they're firmly rooted in a solid strategy. These are the moments that transform passive listeners into active collaborators, skeptics into believers, and ordinary interactions into unforgettable experiences. So, plan your twists, rehearse your

surprises, and then unleash them with confident flair. When you do, you'll not only elevate your message but also spark a connection that lingers long after the moment has passed.

Step up, craft that unique freeze-frame moment, and become the one who commands the stage and captivates every soul in the room. You are the master of the crowd.

Rewind and Reflect Section: Mastering the Element of Surprise

Key Takeaways

- Surprise grabs attention by disrupting expectations and creating memorable emotional spikes.

- Planned spontaneity isn't about chaos—it's about engineering magic that feels organic.

- Unexpected moments build excitement and leave lasting impressions.

- The best surprises serve a purpose: connection, momentum, or message amplification. - True pros know how to read the room and inject spontaneity with strategy, not randomness.

Reflection Questions

- When was the last time a surprise made a lasting impression on you—and why?

- What makes a surprising moment land well versus falling flat?

- How could you engineer spontaneity into your next talk, performance, or meeting?

- What signals can you look for to know when it's time to break from the script?

- How can you use surprise to reengage people when attention begins to dip?

Action Steps

- Add one intentional surprise moment to your next event. Consider a spontaneous shoutout, unexpected transition, or prop.

- Review a past presentation and identify where you could've injected an unexpected twist to boost engagement.

- Brainstorm a list of five simple surprise tactics you can use in your world—from humor to music cues to audience interactions.

Power Concept

Planned spontaneity is a moment in your presentation that is presented to the audience as a spontaneous or on-the-spot, organic moment but is actually prepared and rehearsed.

Chapter 8

Mastering the Close: Dropping the Mic with Impact

"Anyone can start strong, but legends are made in the final seconds."

Anyone can start strong. But legends are made in the final seconds. As we journey through the art of captivating any crowd—from decoding your audience and crafting powerful first impressions to engaging through rebellion, music, and planned spontaneity—we arrive at an essential moment: the art of leaving a lasting impression.

Much like a pastor concluding a sermon that inspires change, the way you finish any interaction holds significant power. It acts as the grand finale, encapsulating your central message and lingering in the minds of your audience long after you've left the room. The beauty of a memorable conclusion lies in its ability to tie everything together, ensuring your presence is felt long after you have exited. It's the final touch that completes the picture and makes your narrative resonate.

This chapter is about mastering that final moment—an opportunity to cement the influence you've built throughout your presentation. Your exit matters whether you're closing a board meeting, a performance, a class, or even a conversation with a friend. The last words or actions you leave behind can echo louder than the content of your entire interaction. The close is where all your preparation, charisma, and audience connection come together for that final punch.

The Power of the Final Moment

Think of it like the final scene in a powerful film—the moment when every emotion, every twist, and every detail comes together in one unforgettable payoff. In the world of crowd engagement, it's no different. The close is where everything you've said and done takes root. It's the emotional crescendo that can either fade into forgetfulness or echo long after the lights come up. A weak ending can unravel the strongest performance. But a well-crafted close? That's what makes a message stick. It's where transformation begins—not in the delivery, but in the departure.

And this truth extends far beyond the stage. Whether you're wrapping a keynote, a classroom lesson, a boardroom pitch, or even a heartfelt conversation at the dinner table, how you close shapes how you're remembered. The final moments don't just summarize—they imprint. When done right, they leave behind more than words. They stir emotion, prompt reflection, and spark action. They become the lasting connection your audience carries with them, long after you've left the room.

Closing with Impact: Techniques for Every Audience

While the importance of a strong close is universal, the way you deliver it depends on the environment, the audience, and your message. Let's explore different ways you can master your closing.

The Personal Touch: Creating Emotional Connection

The most powerful way to end any interaction is to connect on an emotional level. Whether it's through vulnerability, humor, or a poignant personal story, the best closes leave your audience with something they can feel, not just think about. A good closing isn't about saying goodbye.

It's about leaving a piece of yourself behind with your audience.

Take, for example, the ending of a motivational speech. If you want your listeners to feel inspired, don't simply recap your message—deliver a final thought that resonates with their hearts. Use a call to action that feels like a genuine invitation to make a change. When Martin Luther King Jr. closed his famous "I Have a Dream" speech, he didn't simply summarize his points or offer a to-do list. He evoked an emotional response that united the crowd under the banner of hope, justice, and change. His closing wasn't just a conclusion—it was a powerful rallying cry that people remembered for decades.

The emotional connection is particularly crucial when your message is about transformation. Whether you're speaking to inspire, heal, or encourage, the power of your conclusion will hinge on your ability to connect to your audience's deepest emotions. You have to speak to their hearts, not just their minds.

The Call to Action: Leaving No Room for Ambiguity

Sometimes, the best way to close is with a clear, actionable takeaway. In a business context, this could be a call to implement a new strategy. In a classroom, it might involve challenging students to apply the lessons they've learned. A strong call to action turns your speech or presentation into a stepping stone for future action, ensuring that your audience knows exactly what to do next.

In corporate settings, this is where leaders guide their teams toward tangible outcomes. Take the example of Steve Jobs, who often closed his keynote addresses by not just unveiling a product but framing that product as part of a larger movement—something that was changing the world. His call to action was never vague. It was a clear, specific vision of how the audience could be part of the journey ahead.

Similarly, in education, a strong close can encourage students to take their learning into the world. Rather than simply ending a lesson, you can challenge your audience to use the tools you've provided them. This gives your closing purpose and leaves no room for ambiguity. A call to action doesn't just wrap up the talk—it propels it forward.

The Mic Drop: Leaving on a Bold, Unforgettable Note

The mic-drop moment is one of the most iconic ways to end a performance or speech. It's bold and powerful and leaves an indelible mark. But how do you create a mic-drop moment that is earned and not forced? It's all about timing. By this point, you should have built momentum with your content. A well-timed mic drop isn't just about making an abrupt exit—it's about leaving your audience in awe, feeling as if they've just witnessed something truly unique and inspiring. Think of a moment that encapsulates your entire message with clarity, power, and perhaps a touch of surprise.

The key to a mic-drop moment is crafting a close that feels inevitable yet surprising. This is where preparation and spontaneity meet. It's about distilling everything you've said into one final thought or action that feels like a culmination of everything your audience has experienced with you. The audience should feel as if the moment has been building all along, but when it arrives, they're caught off guard by its power. It should bring everything into sharp focus, leaving them with no doubt about the message you've delivered.

A perfect mic drop doesn't need a flashy gesture or dramatic effect. It's the words that matter. Think about a final line that reflects your entire message but feels like a punch to the gut, in the best way possible. It should be something that connects directly to the heart of your audience's emotions, challenging them or inspiring them in a way that feels fresh, powerful, and unforgettable.

Consider a great movie or performance that sticks with you. The best ones don't just have action or humor throughout—

they build to a final moment that elevates everything that came before it. It's the scene where the character experiences a profound realization or the final note of a song that leaves the crowd in silence before they erupt into applause. That's the mic drop.

When you're the host of an event or the speaker on stage, your mic-drop moment should leave your audience feeling as if they've just witnessed something extraordinary. It's not about showing off—it's about making your message resonate at its peak.

The Reflection: Bringing It Full Circle

Another powerful way to close is by revisiting a key moment from earlier in your presentation. This is the art of bringing things full circle. When you end by reminding your audience of the beginning or by tying together earlier themes, you provide closure that resonates deeply.

Consider a TED Talk, for example. The best speakers often begin with a personal anecdote or compelling story that sets the stage for their message. Then, toward the end, they refer back to that same story, completing the arc and providing deeper meaning. This creates a sense of cohesion, making the conclusion feel like a natural progression rather than a sudden end.

The Future Vision: Leaving Them with Hope

When you conclude, it's not just about looking back—it's about pointing forward. The best closings leave the audience excited about what comes next, inspired to take action, or ready to continue the journey you've started together. It's about offering a vision of the future, one that your audience can be part of.

An example of this is seen in many great leaders and visionaries. Think of a political leader closing a campaign speech with a message of hope and unity, inspiring millions to join in the fight for a better tomorrow. It's an invitation to embark on a journey together, where everyone plays a part in shaping what comes next.

This future vision can work in any setting—whether in business, education, or entertainment. A future vision turns the end of your interaction into a beginning, inviting your audience to become part of something larger than themselves.

The Science Behind a Good Close

A good close isn't just effective because it feels powerful—it's backed by science.

Understanding how the brain processes closing moments can help you craft an unforgettable finale.

- **Cognitive closure:** Humans have an inherent need for closure, a concept rooted in gestalt psychology. The brain craves resolution, and it seeks out endings that give meaning to the experiences it has gone through. By delivering a strong close, you provide your audience with a sense of completion and satisfaction. This taps into their psychological need to finish the experience on a positive, resolved note.

- **Recency effect:** Studies in cognitive psychology show that the last thing someone hears or experiences is often the most memorable.[22] This is known as the "recency effect." When crafting a close, take advantage of this by making your final words count. This principle suggests that people will likely remember your closing moment more than anything else you've said, so make sure it resonates deeply.

- **Emotional impact:** Emotion drives memory. When you evoke strong emotions— whether joy, inspiration, or even nostalgia—in your audience, you increase the likelihood that they will remember your message long after the event. Research shows that emotional experiences are

---

[22] Hermann Ebbinghaus, *Memory: A Contribution to Experimental Psychology*, trans. Henry A. Ruger and Clara E. Bussenius (Teachers College, Columbia University, 1913); Lloyd R. Peterson and Margaret J. Peterson, "ShortTerm Retention of Individual Verbal Items," *Journal of Experimental Psychology* 58 (1959): 193–98.

processed in the amygdala, the part of the brain responsible for emotion and memory.[23] By closing on an emotionally charged note, you ensure your message stays with your audience.

- **Call to action:** Great closes also lead the audience to action. Whether they're a subtle call to reflection or a direct call to change, your closing words should push your audience toward some kind of next step. A well-executed call to action signals to the brain that it's time to engage in the next phase, be it reflecting on a message, taking practical steps, or making a decision.

By leveraging these scientific principles, you can create a closing that doesn't just end the conversation—it amplifies your impact and ensures your message endures.

How to Leave a Lasting Impression

Throughout this book, we've explored seven proven strategies for mastering crowd engagement —from decoding your audience to making powerful first impressions, harnessing the power of music, and creating surprise. But, in the end, it all comes down to one key principle: **Be the whistle.**

---

[23] "Amygdala," Cleveland Clinic, last updated April 11, 2023, https://my.clevelandclinic.org/health/body/ 24894-amygdala.

This book has given you the tools to captivate any crowd, but it's the close that truly seals the deal. A great performance, speech, or interaction doesn't end when the content is finished—it ends when you've left your audience with something they can't shake. That's the power of a well-executed close.

Whether you're leading a business meeting, presenting a product, giving a speech, or DJing a crowd, the ultimate goal is to leave your audience transformed in some way. You don't just want them to leave with a sense of "That was good," or "I liked that." You want them to leave thinking, *"That was something I'll remember."*

To do that, you must harness the power of closure: Leave them with something that cuts through the noise and leaves a lasting impression. Be the one they think of when they leave the room. Be the one they tell their friends about. Be the one who inspires them to take action, to change, or to reflect long after your performance is over.

Remember, the best crowd engagers don't just entertain—they inspire, provoke thought, and change the way people feel. They leave their audience with an unforgettable experience, one that will echo in their minds long after the event is over.

And that, my friend, is the power of the close. You are the last thing your audience remembers, so make sure you leave them with something powerful, something that resonates, something that lasts.

Be the whistle.

Rewind and Reflect Section: Mastering the Close

Key Takeaways

- A powerful closing moment solidifies your message and defines how you're remembered.

- Ending with impact isn't about being flashy—it's about being intentional and clear.

- Mic-drop moments come from clarity, emotional resonance, and finality.

- How you close determines whether people feel moved, confused, or inspired.

- A strategic close connects your opening to your message and gives the audience a lasting takeaway.

Reflection Questions

- When was the last time someone's closing words left a lasting impression on you? Why?

- How do you currently end your presentations, and how could you improve it?

- What emotional note do you want to leave your audience with?

- What's your mic-drop move—your signature way to close powerfully and memorably?

- Have you practiced ending with the same energy and intention you begin with?

Action Steps

- Create a one-line summary that encapsulates your core message. Use it as your close. - Practice your closing line as often as your opening. Deliver it with tone, timing, and presence.

- Watch a speaker you admire and analyze how they close. Note what made their close feel final and powerful.

Power Concept

People may forget how you started, but they never forget how you ended.